JN094938

Contemporary
Japanese
History:
since 1945

James M. Vardaman

Higuchi Ken'ichiro

装　　幀＝寄 藤 文 平　垣 内 晴

編集協力＝Michael Brase

写真提供＝共同通信社　毎日新聞社

本書は2009年初版、2013年増補改訂版に新項目を追加した改訂第３版です。
以前の版で書かれた内容は、その時点での史実として残しており、新情報の追加や
データの更新は行っていません。

日本現代史

【改訂第3版】

Contemporary Japanese History: since 1945

James M. Vardaman

ジェームス・M・バーダマン＝著

Higuchi Ken'ichiro

樋口謙一郎＝監訳

はじめに

　本書は、一般読者を念頭において1945年以降の日本の歴史の流れを**概説**することを目指しています。本書を著した動機は30年以上大学で教鞭をとり、現代史について友人や知人と議論を交わすうち、現代の日本人は自身の現代史を全般的に理解していないのではないかという思いを強めたことにあります。高校生や**大学受験者**は、例えば鎌倉時代の出来事、人物、年号はよく知っていても、自分自身が生きる時代、そして彼らの親が生きた時代についてはほとんど知識がないように思えます。大学入試の科目を考えれば、こうした知識を欠くこともおそらく仕方ないでしょう。しかし、われわれの時代に特別な興味を抱かない人は、高校を卒業後に現代について本を読むことなどないかも知れないと思うと、それは痛ましいことです。自分たちの現代史についてもっと知りたいと思う人々のために、本書がその不足を満たす一助になればと願います。

　人は**過去に犯した過ち**から学ばなければ、必ずや過ちを繰り返すという共通の認識があります。歴史を学ぶことのさらに重要な目的は、現在をより的確に理解することなのです。歴史は**静的**ではなく**動的**なものであり、私たちがいるところと私

Preface

This volume is intended for the general reader to give an **overview** of the flow of Japanese history since 1945. It is motivated by a feeling, evolved over more than three decades of teaching university students and discussing recent history with friends and colleagues, that Japanese today do not seem to have an overall understanding of their own contemporary history. While high school students and **university examinees** may be well versed in the events, people and dates of, say, the Kamakura period, they seem to have little knowledge of the period in which they live and in which their own parents lived. Perhaps this lack is inevitable given the subjects of university entrance exams, but it is distressing when one considers that unless a person is particularly interested in our own times, he or she may never read about it after high school. It is hoped that this volume will help to fill the gap for those who want to know more about their own recent history.

It is commonly held that if we do not learn from the **mistakes of the past**, we are destined to repeat them. An even more important reason for learning history is to more adequately understand the present. History is not **static** but **dynamic** and if we are to gain perspective on

たちが向かっているところを総体的に見ようとするなら、**時の流れ**のどこに私たちが今いるのかを多少なりとも把握しておく必要があります。

そのためには、出来事が歴史の空白のなかでただ「起きる」ものではないことを理解しなければなりません。それらの出来事は、誰かが選択し、それらの選択に基づいて行動したがゆえに起きるのです。なぜ私たちがその行為をするかを理解するためには、なぜ過去の人たちが自らの行為をしたかを理解しようと努めることが大切です。

歴史には一つの「正しい」見解などありません。それが本書を著すにあたっての私の基本的な立場です。黒澤明が1950年に制作した映画『羅生門』が示唆するように、実際すべての「事実」は「相対的」なものです。保守主義的、修正主義的、自由主義的、自虐的もしくは理想主義的な歴史観に執着することは、いずれも歴史を**単純にとらえ過ぎる**ことと変わりません。

同様の考え方として、歴史上の「**未解決の問題**」をすべて一連の出来事として整然とまとめてしまうことは、出来事の発生における総体的な混沌をないがしろにし、一つの見方に巧く納まったものだけに着目することです。そうではなく、歴史には多様な見方があり、それゆえに異なる見識を示して「未解決の問題」をひとくくりにするのを避けることが読者にとってより役立つ、というのが私の持論です。日本の現代史を国際的状況に置いて特に日本とは異なる海外の見方を説明し、海外

where we are and where we seem to be going, we need some grasp of where we are in the **flow of time**.

We can do this only if we realize that events do not just "happen" in a historical vacuum. They occur because someone made choices and acted upon them. It is important for us to try to grasp why those people did what they did, if we are to understand why we do what we do.

It is my fundamental stance here that there is no single "correct" view of history. As Kurosawa Akira's 1950 film *Rashomon* suggests, virtually all "facts" are "relative." To cling to a conservative, revisionist, liberal, masochistic or idealistic view of history is to **oversimplify**.

In the same vein, to pull together all the "**loose ends**" of history in some neat chain of events is to ignore the general chaos in which events take place and focus on only those things that fit neatly in one's perspective. Instead, I contend that there are multiple views of history and that we do better service to the reader by showing different views and refraining from attempting to tie the "loose ends" together. Conscious effort has been made to place contemporary Japanese history in the international context, especially describ-

の類似した状況と比較して日本の状況がどうあるかを示すよう意識的に努めました。

　また、歴史の記述にはある程度の主観が必然的に含まれるものであり、それが主題や事件の取捨選択に影響するものです。このため、それらの選択と記述の方法に関する責任は著者にあります。本書は、議論の多い問題については中立的立場にとどまり、考え方の相違を理性的に検討するよう心掛けています。歴史の「解釈」は読者次第であり、その解釈のためには、読者はこうした**簡易版**からできるだけ多くの根拠と見解を得られなければなりません。日本が今どこにいるのかについて、読者が新たな見方を得ることを私は願っています。

注：文中、日本の人名は日本語表記、つまり最初に名字、次に名前の順に記されている。日本語の転記には、著名な地名以外は、ヘボン式を用いている。中国語のローマ字綴りはピンインによる。

---

ing foreign views which differ from Japanese views and showing how the Japanese situation compares with similar situations abroad.

While we might like to claim otherwise, the writing of history necessarily involves a degree of subjectivity, affecting which issues and events one takes up and which one leaves on the sidelines. With this in mind, the author assumes responsibility for both the selection and method of presentation of these matters. The volume tries to remain neutral and give consideration to reasonable differences of perspective on often contentious issues. It is up to the reader to "interpret" history and to do so, he or she must have as much evidence and understanding as is possible in such a **short volume**. I hope that the reader will gain new perspectives on where Japan is today.

第3版のための まえがき

　本書は、2009年に刊行された「日本現代史」の第3版です。初版時より、一つの「正しい」歴史観などというものは存在せず、私たちは自らが生きる世界の全体的な動きを把握するために力を尽くすべきだという**基本的な立場を堅持**しています。2011年3月11日に始まったあの凄惨な悲劇ほど、このことの重要性を**際立たせるものはありません**。あの一連の事件は、いまなお続く問題となっており、また今後数十年にわたって、そうあり続けるでしょう。地震が起きたとき、自分がどこにいたか、その後の日々をどう過ごしたか、この大惨事のイメージがいかに強く私たちの心に残っているか、そして避難し続けている人々や、愛する人を亡くした人々の話が、**いかに耐え難いものであるか**ということを思い起こすことなくして、私たちは、それらの事件を理解することはできないかもしれません。最近起こったこれらの出来事が、思い出し、語り合い、ほかの国々の人々と分かち合う意味のあるものであることに変わりはないのです。

　この第3版が、読者が近い過去を理解しようとし、さまざまな観点からそれを考え、諸外国の人々とこれらの問題を議論するための心構えをする上で役に立てば、というのが著者の願いです。日本を批判したり擁護するのではなく、日本社会の**多様な姿について**の双方向の議論への参画を求めたいと思います。

Preface

This is the third edition of *Contemporary Japanese History*, which first appeared in 2009 and it **maintains the fundamental stance** that there is no single "correct" view of history and that we should do our best to grasp the general dynamics of the world we live in. **Nothing underscores** this better than the overwhelming tragedy that began to unfold on March 11, 2011. Those events remain an issue today and will remain so for decades. We may not be able to interpret those events beyond remembering where we were when the quake struck, how we managed in the days that followed, how powerfully the images of the disaster remain in our minds, or **how unbearable** are the stories of those who still remain displaced or in mourning for missing loved ones. Yet this and other events of our recent past are important to remember, to discuss, and to share with people of other countries.

It is the author's hope that this third updated volume will encourage the reader to understand the recent past, consider it from different perspectives, and be prepared to discuss these issues with people from other countries. This is not a call to criticize or defend Japan, but a call to participate in a two-way discussion about Japanese society **in all its myriad facets**.

目次
Contents

はじめに *Preface* ——— *4*

第3版のためのまえがき *Preface* ——— *10*

日本—1945年 Japan in 1945 ——— *18*

ポツダム宣言 The Potsdam Declaration ——— *20*

生存をかけて Struggling for Survival ——— *22*

占領 Occupation ——— *32*

ダグラス・マッカーサー元帥
    General Douglas MacArthur ——— *34*

軍国主義の排除 Demilitarization ——— *38*

民主化 Democratization ——— *42*

「人間宣言」
    The Declaration of Humanity (*Ningen sengen*) ——— *46*

中心勢力の解体 Decentralization ——— *50*

逆コース Reverse Course ——— *56*

東京裁判 The Tokyo War Crimes Trial ——— *64*

勝利者の裁き? Victor's Justice? ——— *66*

朝鮮戦争の衝撃
    Impact of the Korean Conflict ——— *72*

吉田茂 Yoshida Shigeru ——— *72*

講和条約 Peace Treaty ——— *76*

占領期の映画・文芸作品 Postwar Literature ——— *82*

復興への道のり Hard Work of Recovery ——— *86*

高度経済成長 High-speed Growth ——— *90*

都市生活の変化　Urban Life Transformed ── 92

所得倍増計画　Income-Doubling Plan ── 94

公害　Industrial Pollution ── 98

安保　"Ampo" ── 104

ベトナム戦争と反戦運動
　Vietnam War and the Anti-war Movement ── 106

大学の騒乱　University Upheavals ── 110

東京オリンピック　The Tokyo Olympic Games ── 114

「ニクソン・ショック」　"Nixon Shocks" ── 116

オイルショック　The Oil Shock ── 122

三島由紀夫事件・あさま山荘事件
　Shocks of a Different Sort ── 124

元日本兵の帰国　Return of Yokoi Shoichi (1972)
　and Onoda Hiroo (1974) ── 128

沖縄返還　The Reversion of Okinawa ── 132

貿易摩擦　Trade Friction ── 136

ロッキード事件と田中角栄
　Scandals and Corruption ── 140

公共事業　Public Works ── 146

農村の生活　Life on the Farms ── 148

都市化現象　Urbanization ── 154

サラリーマンと専業主婦　Emergence of the *Sarariiman*
　and Full-time Housewife ── 158

中流日本　Middle-class Japan ── 162

「リッチ・ジャパニーズ」　"Rich Japanese" ── 168

ノスタルジー　Nostalgia ── 170

外国人労働者　Immigrant Labor ── 178

政治の転換　Political Shift ——— *178*

1990年という境界線
The Dividing Line of 1990 ——— *180*

国際社会での動き　International Events ——— *182*

90年代経済問題の教訓
Economic Lessons of the 1990s ——— *188*

自民党の衰退　LDP Decline ——— *194*

改革への道　Road to Reform ——— *200*

中央政府から自治体へ　From Central Government
to Local Government ——— *202*

情報社会の試練
Trials of the Information Society ——— *204*

輸出される日本文化　Cultural Exports ——— *210*

皇位継承問題　The Succession Controversy
of the Imperial Throne ——— *214*

リーマン・ショックと日本経済
Lehman Shock and Japanese Economy ——— *218*

格差社会　Disparate Society ——— *224*

AKB48と芸能界の変化　AKB48 and Changes
in the Entertainment Industry ——— *228*

3.11─地震、津波、そして原発災害　3.11 Earthquake,
Tsunami and Nuclear Disaster ——— *238*

竹島と尖閣諸島をめぐる領土問題　Territorial Dispute over
Takeshima and Senkaku Islands ——— *244*

アベノミクス　Abenomics ——— *248*

COVID-19感染爆発が変えた日常生活
Covid pandemic changes daily life ——— *250*

天皇の退位　The Emperor's abdication ——— *256*

安倍晋三暗殺とその余波　The assassination of Abe Shinzo and its aftermath ——— *258*

大谷翔平が世界的スーパースターに
Ohtani Shohei becomes a worldwide superstar ——— *260*

参考資料　Appendix

日本現代史略年表　A Brief Chronology of Contemporary Japanese History ——— *268*

英語索引　English Index ——— *276*

日本語索引　Japanese Index ——— *280*

参考文献　Bibliography ——— *284*

コラム

1945年 — 英会話のベストセラー	24
サザエさんが取り上げた社会問題	28
ベアテ・シロタ・ゴードンと女性の権利	44
天皇の地方御巡幸	49
『桃太郎』も変わった！	54
下山事件	60
米国のマッカーシズム	62
パール判事	68
「老兵は死なず、ただ消え去るのみ」	76
新幹線開通	116
よど号ハイジャック事件	126
U2偵察機	134
農業の自給自足	152
クマの襲撃	156
食生活の変化	162
国民皆保健	165
ディスコ・フィーバー	168
「不戦決議」と「村山談話」	187
海外に紹介された日本文化	212

過去は死んでいない。それどころか、過去でさえない。

——ウィリアム・フォークナー

The past is not dead. In fact, it's not even past.

——*William Faulkner*

日本——1945年

　1945年8月15日、天皇は自ら日本国民に向けてラジオ放送で発表を行いました。国民は天皇の肉声をこのとき初めて耳にしたのです。天皇は臣民に、「**堪ヘ難キヲ堪ヘ、忍ビ難キヲ忍ブ**」よう求めましたが、多くの人々は、天皇が話していることを正しく理解できませんでした。一つには放送の音質の悪さ、もう一つには発表における格式的な言い回しが原因でした。続いて天皇の言葉についての解説が流れ、発表の趣旨が明らかになりました。戦争が終わり、日本が敗北したのです。日本は**ポツダム宣言**を受諾し「**無条件降伏**」しました。

　しかし別の意味で、日本人はすでに「堪ヘ難キヲ堪ヘ、忍ビ難キヲ忍ブ」道のりを歩み始めていました。

　太平洋戦争の末期、日本は壊滅状態で、**戦闘員210万人**、**民間人70万人**近くの犠牲者、さらに数百万人の病人や負傷者を抱えていました。900万人が住む家を失い、経済は崩壊寸前でした。戦前の最盛期と比較すると、稼働していた工場はわずか4割でした。工業生産は、戦前の1割に落ち込みました。多くの工場が戦火で破壊されたか、さもなくば原料不足で操業を停止していたため、200万人以上が失業していました。運良く職を見つけても、たいていは最低限の賃金しか得られませんでした。インフレが猛威を振るい、どんなに収入を得ても、

Japan in 1945

When the Emperor of Japan announced on August 15 in a radio broadcast—the first time the Japanese people had heard the Emperor's actual voice—that he was asking his people to "**endure the unendurable**," many who heard him did not know exactly what he meant. This was partially due to the static of the broadcast and partly due to the formal language of the announcement. A subsequent explanation of his words made the message very clear: the war was over and Japan had been defeated. Japan had accepted the **Potsdam Declaration** calling for "**unconditional surrender**."

But the Japanese people had already begun "enduring the unendurable" in a different sense.

At the end of the Pacific War, Japan was utterly devastated, with 2.1 million **soldiers** and nearly 700,000 **civilians** dead, millions more ill and wounded. Nine million citizens were homeless and the economy was on the verge of collapse. Compared with the prewar peak, only 40% of factories were able to operate at all. Industrial output was around 10% of prewar levels. With so many factories either destroyed or unable to operate for lack of raw materials, over 2 million workers were without jobs. Those who were lucky enough to find work were usually minimally paid. With rampant inflation, whatever wages they were able to earn bought

市場の商品は次第に買えなくなりました。

　終戦の年には主要都市を執拗に襲った戦略爆撃を逃れて、多くの人々が地方に**疎開**しました。1940年に700万人いた東京の住民は終戦時には300万人に、大阪の住民は300万人から100万人に減少しました。都市部の生活水準も戦前の35%に、少量の作物をかろうじて生産していた農村部でも65%に落ち込みました。都市部が1940年当時の人口を回復するには最低5年はかかると見込まれました。

　日本は全国の富の3分の1と、全所得の半分を失っていました。食物、商品の**価格統制**にもかかわらずインフレーションは激しさを増し、**ヤミ市場の商人**が甘い汁を吸ったのです。軍需物資も一握りの**腐敗官僚**、ヤクザ、産業資本家のふところに消え、一方で庶民は日々の暮らしに困窮していました。

ポツダム宣言

　1945年の7月下旬から8月初旬、ベルリン近郊に位置するポツダムで開かれた**連合国**の最終会談には、ハリー・S・トルーマン（米国）、ヨシフ・スターリン（ソ連）、ウィンストン・チャーチル（英国）が出席しました。各首脳は、中華民国の蒋介石の同意を得て、7月26日、日本政府に対し「**無条件降伏**」を要求し、これ

progressively less in the marketplace.

Many citizens had escaped the sustained strategic bombing of the major cities in the last year of the war in order to **take refuge** in the countryside. Tokyo's seven million residents in 1940 dwindled to three million by war's end, and Osaka went from three million to one million in the same time period. Living standards in cities plummeted to 35% of prewar levels, and to 65% in the countryside, where at least some food could be grown. It would be at least five years before the cities regained their 1940 populations.

Japan had lost one-third of its total wealth and one-half of its total potential income. Inflation soared despite **price controls** on some foods and commodities, making the **black marketeers** rich. Military supplies disappeared into the hands of **corrupt officers**, gangsters and industrialists at a time when ordinary citizens were struggling for daily subsistence.

The Potsdam Declaration

The last conference of the **Allied Powers** in Potsdam (near Berlin) from late July and through August 1945 was attended by Truman (U.S.), Stalin (U.S.S.R.) and Churchill (Great Britain). The leaders, with the approval of Chiang Kai-shek of China, issued a declaration on July 26 calling for Japan to **surrender unconditionally** or face utter destruction. It called for Japan to get

玉音放送を聞く人たち（東京・四谷）
（1945年8月15日）

を受諾しなければ日本は壊滅すると警告しました。宣言は、日本政府に対し、軍部指導者の一掃と新たな政治体制の構築を要求しました。さらに、軍部は解体されなければならないが、日本軍は帰国させるとしていました。また、日本の主権を「本州、北海道、九州、および四国ならびに連合国が決定する諸小島」に限定し、民主的な政府が樹立されるまで連合軍の占領下におく、とされていました。

　日本政府は8月10日、ポツダム宣言の諸条項に基本的に同意しました。それは、ソ連が日本に対して**宣戦布告**をした2日後、長崎に第2の原子爆弾が投下された日の翌日でした。8月14日に宣言の受諾が正式に決定され、8月15日、日本の降伏が天皇によって正式に発表されたのです。

生存をかけて

　終戦の年、都市部は**焼夷弾**を浴び、「**焼け野原**」となりました。日本の工業地帯の約42%が破壊され、大都市の半分以上が焦土と化したのです。終戦当時、爆撃から生き延びた都市住民には住むところもなく、手に入るものは何でも利用してバラックを作りました。彼らは地下蔵や、地面に掘った穴や、地下鉄トンネルに住むか、わずかな板切れを囲って野宿しました。

rid of its militarist leaders and establish a new political order. It further said that Japan's military forces should be disarmed, but allowed to return to Japan. It said that Japan's **sovereignty** would be limited to "Honshu, Hokkaido, Kyushu, Shikoku, and certain smaller islands as we determine" and that Japan would be occupied by Allied forces until it had set up a democratic government.

Japan basically agreed to the terms of the Potsdam Declaration on August 10, two days after the Soviet Union **declared war** on Japan and one day after the second atomic bomb was dropped on Nagasaki. The terms were formally accepted on August 14, and Japan's surrender was formally announced to the Japanese people by the emperor on August 15.

Struggling for Survival

The cities had been razed by **firebombings** in the last year of the war and turned into "**scorched fields**" (*yakenohara*). Some 42% of Japan's urban industrial area had been destroyed and more than half of the total area of the largest cities had been incinerated. At war's end, city dwellers who had survived the bombings build **makeshift shacks** out of whatever materials they could find. They slept in caves, holes in the ground, subway tunnels or in the open with just a few boards to cover them.

雨露をしのぐ場所を見つけるのも大変なのに、食料を手に入れることなど事実上不可能な話でした。当時、1日に必要な最低限度の食事量は約1500キロカロリーと推算されましたが、庶民が実際に摂取していたのはわずか1050キロカロリーでした。戦争終結当時、日本人はすでに**栄養失調**でしたが、平和が訪れても状況は改善されませんでした。

食料と生活必需品の配給——コメ、みそ、しょうゆ、砂糖、香辛料、石けん、ちり紙、マッチ——は、戦時中に始まりました。しかし終戦当時、その**配給制度**は完全に麻痺していました。事実上、庶民は自分のことは自分でなんとかするしかなかったのです。歴史家の色川大吉はこのように回顧しています。「1946年の春、私は兵役を解かれて東京大学に復学した。当時、本郷で下宿先のおかみは、コメ配給の遅

🔖 1945年—英会話のベストセラー

戦後日本での初のミリオンセラーは、終戦直後に生まれました。

天皇がラジオで日本降伏を発表した（玉音放送）その日、編集者の小川菊松は、日本人は、これからやって来る米占領軍兵士との意思疎通が必要になるだろう、と実感しました。彼は特に英語ができるわけではなかったのですが、自分のアイデアを出版社に売り込み、協力者を何人かつのりました。皮肉なことに、日本語部分の編集にあたっては、戦時中に出版された2冊の会話書をモデルにしました。一つは日タイ会話書、もう一つは、日本が中国を占領していた時期に使われていた日中会話書でした。それをもとに東大の学生に英訳させたのです。編集にかかった時間はたったの10日間ほどでした。

こうして玉音放送からわずか1カ月後の9月15日、32頁の英会話書『日米会話手帳』が30万部出版されました。その月の終わりまでには初版部数を売り切り、1945年が終わるまでに実に360万部を売り上げました。

ところが出版直後から紙の価格が高騰したため、出版された年の終わりに

Finding shelter was hard enough, but locating food was virtually impossible. It was estimated that a subsistence diet at that time was about 1,500 kilocalories, but the average citizen was receiving a mere 1,050 per day. At the end of the war, the Japanese people were already **malnourished**, but peace did not improve their situation.

Rationing of food and supplies—including rice, *miso*, soy sauce, sugar, spices, soap, *chiri-gami*, and matches—had begun during the war. But at war's end, the **distribution system** was completely paralyzed. In effect, the ordinary citizen was forced to fend for himself. Historian Irokawa Daikichi recalled, "In the spring of 1946, I was discharged from the army and returned to Tokyo University. During this time, my landlady in Hongo where I had rented a room would often

は出版中止を余儀なくされ、大ヒットにもかかわらず結果は赤字でした。そのベストセラー記録は、1981年に出版されて計700万部を売り上げた『窓ぎわのトットちゃん』(黒柳徹子著)に破られるまで、実に36年間も不動でした。空前のベストセラーを出版した出版社は、紙さえ調達できれば大儲けできたのにと嘆いたのです。

また、1946年2月には、ラジオ番組「カムカム英語」の放送が始まりました。DJ平川唯一氏の名調子と、唱歌「証城寺の狸ばやし」のメロディに番組オリジナル歌詞をのせたテーマソングで大変な人気を博しました。
♪カム カム エブリボディ
　ハウ ドゥ ユウ ドゥー アンド
　ハウ ア ユー……♪

手帳は飛ぶように売れた。日米会話手帳を手に進駐軍と会話する女性（1945年11月）

焼け野原で生活する都民
（1945年5月）

れ—ときには40日も遅れる—を、よくぼやいていた。切羽詰まった私たちは、大学の芝地を掘り起こして芋を植えた。穫れた芋を分け合い、茎も根もすべて残らず料理した。日曜日にはイナゴ捕りに出かけた。」

　1945年、そして1947年にも日本は**肥料不**足、交通・配給の**破綻**から、食料は極めて貴重なものとなりました。コメ生産者は、いくらかでも収穫できたコメを、政府の配給米に供出しませんでした。代わりに農民はコメを隠匿して、物々交換で食料を得ようと都会から足を運ぶ人々に、法外な値段で売りつけたのです。

　現金を持っていた人々は幸運でした。「タケノコ生活」を強いられずに済んだからです。これは、タケノコが何層もの表皮に覆われていることに由来する言葉で、「タマネギの皮」を考えればむしろ分かりやすいかも知れません。実際、人々は、身の回りの品物を一つ一つ売りさばいて食いつなぎ、生きていくしかなかったのです。配給は麻痺し、手に入る品物は**ヤミ市**に流れ、生活必需品の価格は急騰しました。1945年夏の終戦からその年の終わりまでにインフレは6倍、1946年はさらに2.7倍になり、1947年までにさらに3倍となりました。

　「自由市場」「野外市場」「青空市場」などといくら遠回しに呼ばれようと、非公認市場は熾烈な場でした。より正確に言えばそれは「ヤミ市」であり、大都市の「ヤミ」は、売り手

complain about the delays—sometimes up to forty days—in the rationing out of rice. In desperation, we dug up the university lawn and planted yams, which we divided among us and cooked—stems, roots, and all. On Sundays we searched for grasshoppers."

Disastrous harvests in 1945 and again in 1947, lack of **fertilizer**, and **broken-down** transportation and distribution systems made food a highly valued item. Whatever rice farmers were able to produce they avoided turning over to the government, which rationed it to the public. Instead, farmers hid their rice so that they could sell it at exorbitant prices to the city people who came into the country to exchange goods for food.

Those who had cash were the lucky ones. Those who did not faced a *takenoko seikatsu*. While the phrase refers to the layered shoots of new bamboo, it is perhaps easier thought of as an "onion-skin" living. In effect, people were forced to eke out a livelihood by selling off their personal effects one by one in order to survive. With the system of rationing paralyzed and available goods siphoned off onto the **black market**, the cost of daily necessities spiraled upward. From the end of the war in the summer of 1945 to the end of that year, inflation rose six-fold. Between the beginning and the end of 1946, it increased another 2.7 times. Between the beginning and end of 1947, it increased another 3 times.

Whether they were euphemistically called "free markets," "open-sky markets," or "blue-sky markets," the unofficial market for goods was a harsh place. Called more appropriately "black markets" (*yami-ichi*), those

列車で田舎へ向かう買い出
し部隊
（1945年10月）

から「ショバ代」を取り立てるヤクザが牛耳っていました。自然の流れで、売れそうな物を持ち寄る「立ち売り」を始める商人もいました。解雇された工場労働者や元兵士は、持ち逃げできる物はなんでも売りさばきました。農村から運んできた農作物、漁村から運んできた海産物も売られました。

これらの市場は生活必需品を買うだけの場所ではありませんでした。軍の備蓄品だったもの、盗品の機械や建材を買う場所でもありました。これらの資材なくしては町工場の所

⊛ サザエさんが取り上げた社会問題

長谷川町子の漫画「サザエさん」は、サラリーマンの夫と幼い息子を持ち、両親、弟、妹と同居する主婦＝サザエさんとして、今日まで広く親しまれています。しかし1946年にサザエさんが初めて登場したとき、彼女はまだ20歳で、実家に住む独身女性でした。今ではテレビ・アニメ版のおかげで、サザエさんは、デパートのバーゲンに出かけ、同僚と飲みに行く夫のマスオさんを冷ややかに見るごく普通の主婦として知られていますが、昔の漫画では違っていたのです。

鶴見俊輔は、漫画「サザエさん」に登場する社会的なテーマを、1946年と1970年とで比較しています。

1946年のシリーズで取り上げられたテーマは、海外からの引揚者（4回）、占領軍（4回）、買い出し（4回）、自家菜園（3回）、伝染病（2回）、配給（2回）、代用食品（1回）、燃料不足（1回）、ヤミ市（1回）、インフレ（1回）、男女同権の議論（1回）、警察の民主化（1回）、戦争孤児（1回）、復員兵（1回）でした。

1970年には家庭も安定し、結婚して母となったサザエさんは、インフレの影響で家計が苦しくなること以外、あまり世界に関心を向けまていません。鶴見によると、1970年シリーズでのテーマは、大阪万博（7回）、インフレ（4回）、公害（2回）、老齢年金（1回）、子どもの過保護（1回）、経済大国の日本（1回）、主婦のパート（1回）、高い税金（1回）、ゴミ処理（1回）です。

in the major cities were controlled by gangsters, who charged sellers for "**renting a place**" (*shoba dai*). Others started spontaneously with *tachi-uri* (literally "stand and sell") entrepreneurs who had something that others might want. Discharged factory workers and former army soldiers brought whatever goods they could make off with. Sellers brought in food from the country and **sea products** from fishing villages.

These markets were not just places for buying **daily necessities**. They were also places where former military **stockpiles**, stolen machinery and construction supplies could be purchased. Without such materials, the

1970 年代を迎え、日本の一般大衆の象徴としてのサザエさんは、日々の生活に満足し、夫の昇進を必要以上に求めたり、成功を夢見て子どもに勉強を強要したりはしません。サザエさんが食べ物の心配をしなくなったように、実際、日本の家計に占める食費の比率は減少しました。1947 年には、家計の 70% を食費が占めていましたが、1960 年には 44%、1970 年には 34% に減少しています。

つまり、終戦直後は都会でも地方でも、大半の家庭がどん底の生活を強いられていたのです。作物を育てる土地、種、農機具、肥料を持つ農家は多少恵まれていたかもしれません。しかし、都市住民は食卓に最低限の食べ物を並べるのも大変でした。ただでさえ乏しい収入の 70% が食費に消え、住宅や衣類をまかなう余裕などなかったのです。男はたいてい軍服を、女はつぎはぎだらけの木綿服を着ていました。終戦から 4 年を経てようやく、食べ物を買ってもいくらか金銭が残るようになりました。多くの家庭は、そのようにして蓄えたわずかな金銭を子どもの教育に充て、そのほかのことに割く余裕はありませんでした。ほとんどの家庭は貯金を切り崩すか、戦火を免れた家財道具を売りさばくしか、生き延びる手だてはなかったのです。この戦後の厳しさを経験した日本の家族の多くが、1960 年代高度成長期になって、物に困らない生活を送ることができるようになったことを、この上ない喜びと感じたのです。

有者は経営を再建できませんでした。しかし、支払う金額は莫大でした。

庶民にとって、戦後のインフレとヤミ市による最も苦しい要素は、食料供給への影響でした。農作物の生産が戦前の水準を回復するのは1950年代初頭と思われました。その間、栄養失調のために様々な病気が蔓延し、**結核**も流行し始めていました。食料不足が日本に広く打撃を与えたことは、小学生の平均身長・体重が1948年まで減少の一途をたどったことにも示されています。

1946年になると、都市部は食料難で、都市に出入りする列車は自分や家族のために食料を買い出しに出かける人々で混雑しました。大都市近郊の農業地帯に住む農家の女性たちは、コメや野菜などの農作物を入れた籠を背負い、都市に行商に来て、食料の需要に応えました。「かつぎや」として知られた彼女たちは、破壊されずに運行している列車を使ったり、長い距離を歩いたりして、貴重な食料を高価な着物や**家財**、現金と交換しました。都市住民は現金、着物やタバコをかき集め、食料と交換してくれそうな農家が見つかることを祈りつつ、地方に出かけました。

なにより、終戦からほぼ1年半で700万人もの軍人と民間人が海外から帰国しました。終戦時、日本の総人口の10%近くが海外に取り残されていました。軍人370万人と民間人320

owners of small factories could not return to business. But the prices they had to pay were exorbitant.

For the ordinary citizen, the hardest part of post-war inflation and the black market was its impact on food supplies. It would be the early 1950s before agricultural production reached prewar levels again. In the meantime, malnutrition fostered the spread of various diseases and set the stage for an epidemic of **tuberculosis**. Indicative of the broad impact of the food shortage, the average height and weight of elementary school children would decrease until 1948.

Into 1946, there was a serious urban food crisis, and routes to and from the cities were busy with desperate people seeking food for themselves and their families. Farm women from agricultural areas near large cities responded to the need for food by carrying large bundles of rice, vegetables and other farm products onto their backs and bringing them into the city directly to customers. Known as *katsugiya*, these women rode whatever trains had not been destroyed or walked long distances, to barter their precious food supplies for clothing, **heirlooms** and cash. Urban dwellers reversed the route by carrying what cash, kimonos, or cigarettes they could gather onto local trains and traveled out into the countryside in hopes of finding farmers willing to trade these possessions for food.

On top of everything, nearly seven million military and civilian expatriates returned to Japan within a year and a half of the end of the war. When the war ended, nearly 10% of the population of Japan was overseas: 3.7

万人が朝鮮半島、台湾、**満州**地域、中国大陸に散在していました。

　家族や近隣者の期待を背負って出征した人たちは、生還しても、英雄どころか周囲から冷たく扱われました。東条英機首相の下、軍部は「生きて虜囚の辱を受けず」という**戦陣訓**を取り決めていましたが、彼らは生きて帰って来たのです。

　彼らは戦争の敗者として、または新聞で報道され始めていた中国や東南アジアでの**残虐行為**を手掛けた者と見なされました。父や息子を戦場に送った家族もほとんど同情されず、軍の支給金も届きませんでした。引き揚げてきた民間人も、「祖国」に戻っても疎外感を抱いていました。所持品もわずかで、さらに財産もほとんど持たずに帰国した彼らは、哀れみの入り交じった目で見られ、また他国に対する失敗した**植民地経営**に加担したと軽蔑されていたのです。

占領

　連合国は、戦争が継続中だった1942年から戦後の対日占領計画に着手していました。当初の計画では、3年の占領で民主化によって日本を**非軍国主義化**させ、大日本帝国を解体し、憲法を改正し、財閥を解体し、政府と神道

million soldiers and 3.2 million civilians scattered over Korea, Taiwan, **Manchuria** and the Chinese mainland.

Those who had gone off to the battlefields with the best wishes of their families and neighbors often found that they were treated as less than heroes upon their return. Under Prime Minister Tojo, the army had issued a famous **field code** in which all fighting men were encouraged to "not live to incur the shame of becoming a prisoner," but these men were returning alive.

Either they were treated as losers, or as men who had committed the **atrocities** in China and Southeast Asia that were just beginning to be described in the newspapers. The families that had sent off their fathers and sons received little sympathy and military paychecks were no longer arriving regularly in the mail. Repatriated civilians also felt out of place when they returned "home." They were regarded with a mixture of pity because they had few possessions and fewer financial resources and scorn for playing a role in the failed **colonization** of other nations.

Occupation

The Allied nations had begun planning for the postwar occupation of Japan since 1942, while the war was still on. Originally they had considered a three-year occupation which would **demilitarize** Japan through democratization, dismember the Japanese empire, revise the

を断絶させることを想定していました。しかし、これらの課題を実現するのに要する期間を早期に推算していたにもかかわらず、実際の占領は6年以上に及びました。戦争中の同盟国だったドイツが米国、フランス、英国、ソ連の4カ国に分割占領されたのとは対照的に、日本は米国一国に占領されることとされました。

ダグラス・マッカーサー元帥

　1945年8月30日、ダグラス・マッカーサー元帥は東京の南西に位置する厚木基地に降り立ちました。マッカーサーは、武器を身に付けず、ワイシャツ姿で専用機から姿を現したときにはすでに、かつての敵国の地での**改革の実行**について、いくつかのことを決断していました。

　数日後の9月2日、日米両政府の代表は、東京湾に浮かぶ米戦艦ミズーリ号に乗船し、**降伏文書**に正式に調印しました。甲板には二つの米国旗が掲げられました。一つは、1世紀前に日本に来航し、鎖国政策を終わらせたペリー提督の旗艦に翻っていた星31個の星条旗でした。もう一つは、1941年に**真珠湾**が攻撃された日の朝、ワシントンのホワイトハウスに翻っていた星条旗でした。

厚木飛行場に降り立つマッカーサー元帥
（1945年8月）

Constitution, dissolve the *zaibatsu* conglomerates and dissolve the connections between the government and Shinto. Despite the earlier estimate of the time it would take to accomplish these goals, the Occupation would actually last more than six years. In contrast with its wartime ally Germany—which was occupied by the U.S., France, Great Britain and the Soviet Union—Japan would be occupied by the Americans.

General Douglas MacArthur

On August 30, 1945, General Douglas MacArthur arrived at Atsugi Air Base, south west of Tokyo, and when he emerged from his aircraft unarmed and in shirtsleeves, he had already decided several things about how he would **implement changes** in the land of the former enemy.

Several days later, on September 2, representatives of the Japanese and American government met on board the *USS Missouri* in Tokyo Bay to sign the official **surrender**. On the deck were two American flags. One was the 31-star flag that had flown on the mast of Commodore Perry's ship when he arrived in Japan about a century earlier, ending the Japanese policy of national seclusion. The other was the flag that had hung over the White House in Washington, D.C., on the morning **Pearl Harbor** was attacked in 1941.

米国大使館公邸で行われた
歴史的会談後のマッカーサ
ーと昭和天皇
（1945年9月29日）

　　連合国軍最高司令官に任命されたマッカー
サーは、米国から来た将軍であるかのように
権力を行使しました。彼の総司令部は、皇居の
向かいに位置し、東京大空襲の戦火を逃れた
数少ない西洋式建物の一つだった第一生命ビ
ルに設置され、マッカーサーの「城」からは皇
居の堀が一望できました。

　　天皇の側近が、マッカーサーに対して皇居
に出向いて天皇と会見するよう提案すると、逆
にマッカーサーは、旧米国大使館内の公邸に天
皇を呼び出しました。両者の初対面を撮影した
有名な写真は、誰が勝者で、誰が敗者であるか
をはっきりと映し出していました。それまで日
本国民は、天皇の威厳のある姿をとらえた写真
しか見たことがなかったため、この新たな写真
は相当な衝撃でした。若い天皇が、会見用の**礼
装に身を包んで**右側に緊張して立ちました。日
本の事実上の新統治者は、カーキ色の**開衿ミリ
タリーシャツ**を着て、勲章を一切つけず、腰に
手をあてて実にリラックスした面持ちで左側
に立っていました。この写真が天皇の完全な**従
属**を象徴していると解釈した人もいましたが、
別のメッセージを読み取った人もいました。そ
れは、天皇はマッカーサーという後ろ盾を得
て、戦後の日本においても何らかの役割を果た
すだろうというものでした。

　　それぞれの立場は明確でしたが、米国政府
から下されたマッカーサーの指示は間接的な
方法で日本を占領することでした。最高司令
官は日本を直接支配するのではなく、残存す

As **Supreme Commander of the Allied Powers** (SCAP), MacArthur would wield power like an American shogun. His headquarters located in the Dai-Ichi Insurance Building, just opposite the Imperial Palace and one of a very few Western-style buildings that survived the bombing of Tokyo, MacArthur's "castle" towered over the **moat** surrounding the palace.

When advisers to the emperor suggested that MacArthur come to the palace to meet the emperor, MacArthur instead summoned the emperor to the general's official residence, in the former U.S. embassy building. The famous photograph of their first encounter makes it very clear who was the victor and who was the defeated. In the past, the public had only seen photographs of the emperor that projected his august personage, so this new photograph came as somewhat of a shock. The younger emperor standing stiffly on the right is carefully **dressed in tails** for the occasion. The new de facto ruler of Japan, wearing an **open-necked** military khaki shirt with no medals, stands casually with his hands on his hips on the left. While some interpret the photo as symbolic of the emperor's complete **subservience**, others detected in the photo another message: the emperor would have a role to play in postwar Japan, with the backing of MacArthur.

Despite the clarity of their respective positions, MacArthur's orders from Washington were to maintain an occupation of Japan through indirect means. Instead of a direct rule of the country, SCAP was to make use of

連合国軍最高司令官総司令部（GHQ）
英語での正式名称は、General Headquarters/Supreme Commander of the Allied Powers です。略語は、GHQ/SCAP が用いられています。「GHQ」は日本国内のみでの通称で、米国では「GHQ」のみでは意味が通じないことがあります。
　本書では、GHQ/SCAPの日本語訳として「GHQ」を使っています。

る日本の**官僚機構**を活用して占領せよ、というものでした。マッカーサーをトップとして米国人約5000人で構成されたGHQは、日本の政府機構に基本的に沿った機関に区分されました。日本人官僚を管理・指示したのはこれらGHQの各機関でしたが、重要なのは、その指示を実際に遂行したのはほかでもない日本人官僚だったということです。

　戦後の日本政府が行った改革はすべてマッカーサーが手掛けたと決めてかかるより、マッカーサーを変化と改革の**触媒**と見る方がおそらくより正確でしょう。歴史家の色川大吉が「米国が日本を改革したとはいえない。GHQは改革の機会を日本に提供しただけだ。彼らの貢献は、改革を阻むものを破壊したということだ」と述べるように。この点をふまえて、占領期に行われた実際の改革を見ていくことにします。

軍国主義の排除

　マッカーサーが断行した最も露骨な変革は、日本の植民地主義的帝国と軍部の**解体**でした。

　日本は1895年に台湾を、1910年に朝鮮をそれぞれ**併合**することによって、帝国を築きました。第2次世界大戦のまっただなか、大日本帝国は、東はほぼハワイ諸島に及ぶ太平洋、西は

the Japanese **bureaucracy** which was to be left in place. The SCAP General Headquarters (GHQ), composed of some 5,000 Americans under MacArthur, was divided into agencies that essentially paralleled the Japanese government structure. It was these agencies that would oversee the Japanese bureaucrats and give them instructions, but significantly, it was the Japanese bureaucrats who carried out the instructions.

Rather than assume that all the changes in postwar Japanese government were instituted by SCAP, it is probably more accurate to see SCAP as a **catalyst** for change and reform. As the historian Irokawa Daikichi writes, "It cannot be said that the United States reformed Japan. GHQ simply provided Japan with the opportunity to carry out reforms. Their gift was the destruction of the obstacles that had stood in the way of reform." With this in mind, we turn to the actual reforms implemented in Japan during the Occupation.

Demilitarization

The most obvious change that MacArthur implemented was the **dismantling** of Japan's colonial empire and its military forces.

Japan had launched its empire by **taking over** Taiwan (Formosa) in 1895 and Korea in 1910. At its height in the middle of World War II, the empire stretched east into the Pacific almost to Hawaii, west to eastern

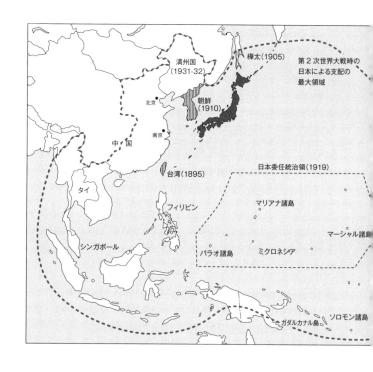

中国東部、ビルマ、南はインドネシア、ニューギニア島とパプア、そして北は満州国、樺太に及びました。GHQが最初に手掛けたことの一つとして、これらの領土や**委任統治領**をすべて日本から剥奪し、日本の領土を、1868年の**明治維新**当時の北海道、本州、四国、九州の4島に戻しました。

　帝国陸軍・海軍は速やかに解体され、GHQは旧日本兵の帰還という長期に及ぶ作業に着手しました。政治的な非軍国主義化も、公職、警察、新聞、政治団体から軍国主義者と国粋主義者を**追放する**という形で行われました。こ

公職追放
1946年（昭和21年）に施行された「公職追放令」です。戦争犯罪人、戦争協力者などが公職を追われました。主な追放者には鳩山一郎、徳富蘇峰、正力松太郎などがいます（第1次公職追放）。その後、労働運動の激化に伴いGHQは占領政策を転換し、共産主義者を主な対象としました（レッド・パージ）。この政策は、1952年のサンフランシスコ平和条約発効と同時に廃止されました。

40

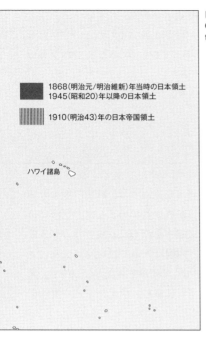

日本帝国の領土の変遷
Changes in the Territories within
the Japanese Empire

■ 1868（明治元/明治維新）年当時の日本領土
1945（昭和20）年以降の日本領土

||||| 1910（明治43）年の日本帝国領土

ハワイ諸島

China and Burma (Myanmar), south to Indonesia, New
Guinea and Papua, and north to Manchukuo (Manchuria) and Karafuto. As one of its first acts, SCAP stripped
Japan of all its territories and **mandates** and left it with
just the four main islands that it had begun with in 1868
at the time of the **Meiji Restoration**.

The Imperial Army and Navy were quickly abol-
ished and SCAP began the long process of bringing
ex-military personnel back to Japan. Political demilitarization also took the form of **purging** militarists
and nationalists from public office, police forces,

の追放を**やり過ぎ**だと思った日本人も、手ぬ
るいと思った日本人もいました。いずれにせ
よ、1948年半ばまでに約20万人が職を失い
ました。

民主化

　戦前の対日占領計画では、政治制度の大胆
な改革に焦点が置かれていました。憲法は市
民的自由を保障するために改正されるべきと
されました。**内閣**は天皇ではなく**立法府**に従
うことになりました。政府は天皇ではなく、国
民にその権限が由来し、国民に対して責任を
負うとされました。

　日本の官僚機構を通して憲法の改正を進め
ようとしていたマッカーサーは、この指針を
満たす改正草案を作成するよう日本の政治指
導者たちに強く求めました。一方で、有力な
新聞や民間人も自発的に憲法案を提起しまし
た。それらの案は、天皇主権を維持し、従来の
憲法を単に表面的に修正しただけの案から、
まったく新しい憲法を制定する案まで様々で
した。最終的に、日本の指導者たちから提起さ
れた**憲法改正案**は、マッカーサーにとってまっ
たく受け入れ難いものでした。代わりに彼は、
GHQスタッフからなる作業チームに憲法の
「モデル」を、それも1週間以内に作成するよ
うに命じました。

newspapers and political groups. Some Japanese saw these purges as **going too far** and others saw them as not going far enough. Regardless, by the middle of 1948 some 200,000 people had lost their jobs.

Democratization

Prewar planning for the Occupation of Japan was centered on a massive restructuring of the political system. The constitution was to be revised to guarantee civil liberties to the people. The **cabinet** would answer to the **legislature**, not to the emperor. The government would derive its authority from and be responsible to the people, not to the emperor.

Intending to work through the Japanese bureaucracy in altering Japan's constitution, MacArthur pressed the leadership to draft revisions that would incorporate the above guidelines, while on their own initiative newspapers and private citizens joined in making their own proposals. The proposed changes varied between maintaining **imperial sovereignty** and only superficially changing the existing constitution and completely relocating sovereignty with the people and enacting an entirely new constitution. In the end, the **proposed constitutional changes** brought forth by Japanese leaders were entirely unacceptable to MacArthur. Instead, he assigned a task force of GHQ staff members to draw up a "model" constitution—and to do so within

この条文の作成を任されたスタッフは、日本人を処罰するような立場は取らず、日本人が自らの社会を築くことを認める、より民主的で**平等主義的**だとの考えに至った草案を作成しました。

何よりもまず、天皇から主権を剥奪し、天皇を「日本国の象徴であり、日本国民統合の象徴」と定め、かわりに国民に主権を付与しました。第2に、国家神道を廃止し、政府が宗教教育をはじめとする宗教活動を行うことを禁止しました。第3に、男女平等を唱え、女性に参政権を付与しました。第4に、長年議論が膠着化している**第9条**のなかで「日本国民は、……国権の発動たる戦争と、武力による威嚇又は武力の行使は、国際紛争を解決する手段としては、永久にこれを放棄する」とされ、「陸海空軍その他の戦力は、これを保持しない」と付け加えられました。

ベアテ・シロタ・ゴードンと女性の権利

GHQの憲法草案作成グループには、日本での実体験に基づく知識を持つスタッフが一人だけいました。22歳のユダヤ系女性のベアテ・シロタ・ゴードンでした。ウィーン生まれの彼女は、ピアニストの父が東京音楽学校（現在の東京芸術大学）で教えていたことから、少女時代を日本で過ごしました。日本のアメリカンスクールを終えると米国の大学に進学、その後、政府関係の仕事に就きました。戦後、再来日した彼女は、GHQの民政局で日本政治と女性問題を調査する仕事を得ました。

彼女は、日本人女性、子ども、芸術家、知識人と接した幼少期の経験を通じて、戦前の日本では、政治・法制度の下で個人の自由が制限されているこ

a period of a single week.

The men and women who were pressed into drawing up this document did not take a punitive stance toward the Japanese, but wrote what they thought would create a more democratic and **egalitarian** document that would allow the Japanese to build their own society.

First and foremost, it deprived the emperor of sovereignty and made the monarch "a symbol of the State and of the unity of the people" and placed sovereignty in the hands of the people. Second, it separated Shinto religion from the State, not allowing the government to participate in religious education or other religious activity. Third, it extended the vote and equal rights to women. Fourth—a sticking point through the years—in **Article 9**, it said that "the Japanese people forever renounce war as a sovereign right of the nation and the threat or use of force as a means of settling international disputes" and added that "land, sea, and air forces, as well as other war potential, will never be maintained."

とを強く認識するようになりました。憲法改正作業に参加した彼女は、より抑圧の少ない社会をつくりたいという思いを抱いていました。彼女は、それこそが政治指導者から得られなかった日本の大衆の願いだと感じていました。ベアテ・シロタの多大な貢献によって、GHQ憲法草案作成グループは、「両性平等の原則」にも同意しました。皮肉なことに、合衆国憲法にもこれを保障するとは明示されていません。実にそれは、近代法において最も力強い男女同権の条項の一つでした。

結局、いわゆる「マッカーサー草案」として知られるこの原案は、ほとんど修正されずに国会で承認され、1947年5月3日に**施行されました**。振り返ってみると、皮肉なことに、日本の憲法は、公衆衛生と社会福祉の増進、労働組合の団体交渉権、すべての国民が「**健康で文化的な最低限度の生活を営む権利**」を保障しているという意味で、合衆国憲法よりも進歩的なのです。世界的に見ると、「平和条項」として知られる第9条には、卓越した特徴があります。ほかの近代国家は、国家の「主権」として、戦争を放棄したことがないからです。

「人間宣言」

　1946年1月1日、天皇はGHQの意向を受けて、後に「**人間宣言**」として知られる詔書を新聞紙上に発表しました。国民は天皇を「現御神（あきつみかみ）」と考えるべきではない、と天皇が宣言したのです。

　日本の新内閣とマッカーサーは、この詔書によって新たな局面を開き、天皇のイメージを**回復**させようとしました。しかしこの詔書が意味することについての両者の解釈は大きく異なっていました。マッカーサー——そして西洋諸国——は、天皇が国民に向けて率直に、

Eventually the so-called MacArthur draft, with minor revisions, was approved by the National Diet and **took effect** on May 3, 1947. **In retrospect,** it is ironic that the Japanese Constitution is in many ways more liberal than the U.S. Constitution in guaranteeing the promotion of public health and social welfare, the rights of workers to bargain collectively with employers and the right of everyone "**to maintain the minimum standards of wholesome and cultured living.**" From a world perspective, the prominent characteristic is Article 9, known as the "peace clause," for no other modern government had ever renounced war as a "sovereign right" of the nation.

The Declaration of Humanity (*Ningen sengen*)

On January 1, 1946, the emperor, with the prompting of GHQ, issued to the press a **rescript** that came to be known as his "**Declaration of Humanity.**" The emperor declared that the people should not consider him to be *akitsu-mikami* ("a living deity").

Both the new Japanese cabinet and SCAP intended to use this rescript to open a new phase in a campaign to **rehabilitate** the image of the emperor. But their respective takes on what the rescript meant were quite different. To SCAP—and the Western world—the emperor had said straightforwardly that his people were

自らを「現人神」と考えてはならないと述べたのだから、天皇は、自らがイエス・キリストのような——西洋的な意味での——神の生ける子ではないと言いたかったのだと考えました。

　ところが実際には、天皇は自らが天照大神の子孫であることを無条件に否定したわけではありませんでした。つまり、否定した**神格性**の根源であるその**神話**について、天皇は一切触れなかったのです。それゆえ、この解釈をめぐり、日本人と他の国々の人々の間で解釈の違いが常に存在してきました。しかし、明白にされているのは次の点です。「私とあなたたち臣民との間の絆は、いつもお互いの信頼と敬愛によって結ばれ、単なる神話と伝説によって生まれたものではない。天皇は現人神、日本国民はほかより優れた民族で、ひいては世界の支配者たるべく運命づけられたという架空の概念に基づくものではない」。

天皇地方巡幸　熊本市慈愛園
にて（1949年）

not to think of him as "a living deity," assuming that he meant he was not a living son of God—in the Western sense—like Jesus Christ.

But in actuality, he was not unconditionally denying descent from the Sun Goddess, Amaterasu Omikami. In short, he had left intact the **myth** that was the basis of his renounced **divinity**. Hence, there has always been a gap between what the Japanese and other peoples think about this declaration. What is clear, however, is the following: "The ties between me and my people have always been formed by mutual trust and affection. They do not depend upon mere legends or myths. Nor are they predicated on the false conception that the emperor is divine, and that the Japanese are superior to other races and destined to rule the world."

🏯 天皇の地方御巡幸

人間宣言をした1946年2月、天皇の地方御巡幸が始まりました。「神」ではなく同じ人間として、国民の中に分け入って同じ目線に立ちました。その後、1954年8月に終了するまで、沖縄を除く全国の都道府県すべてに足を運び、全行程合わせて3万3000キロに渡る巡幸となりました。戦災にあった子どもや、工場で働く職工さんを訪ねたりして国民との交流に努めました。天皇が国民との会話のなかでよく使った「アッ、ソウ」という独特の言い回しは、ちょっとした流行の言葉となりました。

中心勢力の解体

占領政策の第3の目的は、軍部と産業エリートへの勢力の集中を**解体**し、改革に寄与する新たな勢力を**育てる**ことでした。

第1に、**財閥の解体**が実施されました。GHQは、財閥が軍部と結託して帝国を海外に拡張し、戦争を引き起こしたと考えました。これら複合企業体の解体によってのみ、民主主義が支障なく育つと考えられました。

第2に、労使間の**収入分配**をより適切に行う手段として、労働組合が奨励されました。労働条件を改善し、賃金を引き上げることで、GHQは経済的により自立的な**中産階級**を築き、その階級が改革を推進すると考えました。

第3に、GHQは**農地改革**を実施しました。終戦当時、総人口の約半分が依然として**農村**に居住しており、農村部の貧困は深刻な経済的、社会的問題でした。戦前にも日本政府が農地改革を提起したことがありましたが、実現できませんでした。GHQは、民主主義を築き、**不在地主**と実際に土地を耕作する**小作農**との経済力の格差をなくすためには、経済的平等が不可欠だと考えました。GHQは、不在地主と在村地主から土地を没収し、実際に土地に住んで耕作した小作農に適正な価格で土地

財閥解体
1946年9月から翌47年9月までの約1年間で、三井、三菱、住友、安田の4大財閥と新興コンツェルンや地方財閥、小規模財閥などを含む83の会社が解体の指令を受けました。

Decentralization

A third goal of the Occupation was to **dissolve** the concentrations of influence of the military and industrial elites and to **foster** the growth of new groups that would work toward reform.

The first step involved **breaking up the industrial conglomerates** (*zaibatsu*) which SCAP believed had conspired with the military to expand the Japanese empire overseas, initiating the war. Only with the dismantling of these conglomerates would democracy be allowed to grow freely.

Second, labor unions were promoted as a means of creating a better **distribution of income** between employers and employees. By improving working conditions and raising wages, SCAP hoped to create a more independent **middle class** that would promote the reforms.

Third, SCAP implemented **rural land reforms**. At the end of the war, almost half of Japan's population still resided in **agricultural villages**, and rural poverty remained a serious economic and social problem. Even before the war, the Japanese government had proposed land reforms but had never been able to implement them. SCAP saw economic equality as essential to building democracy and eliminating the gap between the economic power of **absentee landlords** and the **tenant farmers** who actually farmed the land. It ordered the Japanese government to confiscate land from both

を売却するよう、日本政府に命じました。

　1946年の農地改革法の施行により、政府が不在地主が所有するすべての土地を買い上げることが認められました。さらに、在村地主には、自らの労働力で耕せるだけの土地を所有することが認められました。これは、ほぼすべての県で各々2.5エーカー、北海道では例外的に10エーカーと見積もられました。**中央政府**が土地を買い上げた後、旧小作農に一律価格で転売しました。政府は230万人の地主から数百万エーカーの土地を買い上げ、470万人の農家に、30年間以上に渡り利率3.2%という破格の条件で売却しました。この**経済的再編**の影響は驚異的なものでした。1950年までに全国の**水田**の90%近くを居住所有者が耕作し、極めて低い価格で土地の所有権を得ていました。その結果、旧地主は富だけでなく村内での地位まで失い、独立農民という新たな階層が生まれました。旧地主が不満を抱いてもおかしくなかったのですが、大局的に見れば、占領によって実施された改革のなかでも農地改革は最も効果的なものでした。

　第4に、教育政策における集権化された官僚の権限が縮小されました。1946年3月、米国の教育使節団が来日し、日本中の学校を調査しました。彼らは、学校の管理を極度に集権化せずに、むしろ広く分散させることを基本原則とする**提言**をまとめました。

absentee and resident landowners and sell the land at reasonable prices to the tenants who lived on and worked the land.

The Farm Land Reform Law of 1946 permitted the government to purchase all lands belonging to absentee landlords. Further, it permitted resident landlords to keep only as much land as their families could cultivate with their own labor. In most prefectures this amounted to 2.5 acres, with the exception of 10 acres in Hokkaido. The **national government** bought the land then resold the land to former tenants at that identical price. The government purchased millions of acres from 2.3 million landowners and resold it to 4.7 million cultivators on easy terms, 3.2% interest over 30 years. The impact of this **economic reshuffle** was tremendous. By 1950, resident-owners cultivated nearly 90% of all **paddy fields** in the country, and they had obtained title on the land at extremely low prices. As a result, the former landlords lost not only their wealth but also their status within the villages and a new broad class of independent farmers came forward. Former landowners had legitimate reason to grumble, but by most estimates, land reform was the most successful of the reforms introduced by the Occupation.

Fourth, centered bureaucratic control over education was significantly reduced. A mission of American educators visited Japan in March 1946 and traveled throughout the country inspecting schools. They prepared a set of **recommendations** based on the principle that control of the schools should not be highly centralized

その改革案では、住民によって選出した教育委員会を都道府県に設置し、教師を選択し、使用する教科書を選定し、カリキュラムを設定することが提案されました。戦前のエリート主義的な複線型学制ではなく、米国式の単線型学制により小学校6年、中学校3年、高校3年とすることになりました。この「6–3–3制」の導入によりGHQは、教育の機会を拡大するとともに教育内容を充実させたいと考えました。

1947年制定の**教育基本法**では、教育の目的は従来のように国家に仕えることではないことが明確にされました。**個人の尊厳**を重んじ、平和と真理を希求する人間の育成を期するためのものとされたのです。

教育の変化は、驚愕と当惑を呼ぶものでした。**最優先**とされたのは学校の再開でしたが、手に入る教科書といえば、軍国主義的価値観を打ち出した戦前の教科書だけだったのです。手に入るものを最大限に活用するために、特に歴史、倫理、地理の教科書のうち、不適格な部分は**墨塗り**され、ページがすべて真っ黒に塗りつぶされていることもありました。愛国的理念を説き、教え子を戦場に送った教師は、自

黒塗りの教科書

🍑『桃太郎』も変わった！

　教育における大きな変化は、戦後、おとぎ話の解釈が変わったことからも見て取れます。戦時中、『桃太郎』は、愛国心の強い英雄が悪魔（西洋）と戦い、国を征服から救う話として読まれていました。その労苦の見返りとして、彼は戦果の宝物を持ち帰りました。ある教師によると、戦後

but rather widely dispersed.

Among the reforms proposed was to establish prefectural school boards elected by the residents, to choose teachers, decide what textbooks would be used, and set forth the curriculum. Rather than the prewar elitist multitracking system, an American-style single-track system would include 6 years of elementary school, 3 years of junior high school and 3 years of high school. By introducing this "6–3–3 system," SCAP hoped to expand the content of education as well as increase access to it.

The 1947 **Fundamental Law of Education** declared that the goal of education was not to serve the nation, as it had been until that date. Rather it was to promote **individual dignity** and work to instill a love for peace and truth.

The changes in education were startling and confusing. **Priority** was given to reopening schools, but the only textbooks available were the prewar books which promoted militaristic values. In an effort to make use of what was available, unacceptable passages especially in the history, ethics and geography textbooks were **blackened out**, which meant in some cases full pages were covered in black ink. Teachers who had formerly promoted patriotic ideals and sent their students off to the

の授業では子どもの関心は英雄でも悪魔でもなく、もっぱら宝物に向けられたそうです。あるクラスでは、宝物はおそらく金か食べ物だから、均等に分けて貧しい人にあげるべきだ、という意見を述べた児童もいたそうです。

らがしてきたことを誇れず、生徒の信頼をず
いぶん失いました。平和、民主主義、文化を目
指す新しいカリキュラムでは、新しい教師、あ
るいは少なくとも今までの教師の思想の改革
が必要とされたのです。

逆コース

　変化があるという発表はなかったものの、
1947年になるとGHQの政策には転換が表れ、
それは「逆コース」と呼ばれるほど**あからさま**
でした。まる2年間の改革を経て、日本の人々
の変化への情熱に翳りが見え始め、経済と政
治をめぐる問題は増える一方でした。政策転
換の**契機**の一端は国内的なものでした。経済
は依然として再編を必要とし、労働組合は収
拾がつかなくなっていました。そして日本は
何らかの形で国際社会に再び参画することを
求められていました。

　外的な契機は、特に東アジアで活発化して
いた国際共産主義の台頭でした。二つの朝鮮
の対立により、多くの米国の指導者は、自国の
政策の遂行のためには、東アジアにおける共
産主義のさらなる拡大を阻む、安定的で民主
的な日本が必要だと考えました。日本が政治
的に安定するには経済復興が必要だと、彼ら
は感じていました。**端的に言えば**、米国の政策
目標は、日本が速やかに太平洋地域における

battlefront were no longer proud of what they had done and lost a considerable degree of respect in the eyes of their students. A new curriculum aimed at peace, democracy and culture would require new teachers, or at least a reform of the thinking of the present teachers.

Reverse Course

While there was no declaration that change was about to occur, beginning in 1947 there was a shift in SCAP policy that was **distinct** enough to earn the label "the reverse course." Two full years of reform had left Japan with declining enthusiasm for change and mounting problems in economics and politics. Part of the **impetus** for this turnabout was internal. The economy needed reconstructing, labor unions were getting out of control, and Japan was being called to rejoin the community of nations **in some manner**.

The external impetus was the **rise** of international **communism**, which seemed particularly active in East Asia. Hostility between the two Koreas persuaded many U.S. leaders that the implementation of U.S. policy required a stable, democratic Japan capable of preventing the further spread of communism in East Asia. A politically stable Japan, they felt, required an **economic revival**. The U.S. policy goal, **plainly stated**, was for Japan to quickly become America's ally in the Pacific.

米国の同盟国になることでした。

　この目標の達成には、勢いを増す労働組合運動を規制し、財閥の解体を中止することが必要とされました。財閥は単に愛国的な存在だったのであり、アジアや太平洋へ軍事的拡張を推進したわけではないという新たな見方が提起されました。これらの財閥を撤廃することは何ら良い結果を生まない。それどころか、これらの大企業は日本経済の復興に必要な存在だ、というわけです。

　こうしたことから、労働組合に対する考え方は完全に変わりました。終戦直後の不安定な労働条件の問題に対峙した労働組合は1946年末までに早くも約480万人の組合員を集めていました。組合員の大半は、純粋に、家族を養うに十分な収入と雇用の保障に関心を寄せていました。しかし、**共産主義支持者**は労働運動に政治的課題も持ち出したのです。GHQは日本の官僚集団と同様に、組合が過激なストライキを起こし社会の混乱を招くことを憂慮しました。当時、日本経済には新たな問題に対処できる余力などありませんでした。占領政策の主眼が民主化から経済成長へと移ったことは、GHQによる1947年のゼネスト禁止に示されていました。

　「逆コース」の一端として、日本の指導者たちは労働者を締め付け、経営者側を支援し始めました。その結果、当初追放された人々の多くが1949年までには復権し、1950年には第2の追放――「レッド・パージ」――が始まりま

二・一ゼネスト
占領政策により次第に勢いをます労働組合に対し、1947年1月1日、総理大臣の吉田茂は年頭の辞で、組合を「不逞の輩」と発言しました。それに反発して、各組合が次々とゼネラルストライキの実施を決定。2月1日を実施日と決めていましたが、前日にGHQがゼネストの中止を指令しました。

To achieve that goal required restraining the rising labor movement and bringing to a halt the breaking up of the *zaibatsu*. The conglomerates, according to the new view, had merely been loyal patriots and had not advanced military expansion into Asia and the Pacific. To abolish these conglomerates, therefore, served no positive end. To the contrary, these industrial giants were necessary to revitalize the Japanese economy.

This led to a complete change in attitude toward labor unions. Faced with precarious working conditions in the immediate postwar days, labor unions had quickly gathered a membership of some 4.8 million workers by the end of 1946. The vast majority of members were concerned simply about earning enough to support their families and gaining **job security**. But **pro-Communists** within the labor movements brought out a political agenda as well. SCAP as well as the Japanese bureaucracy were concerned that the unions would bring on disruptive strikes that would lead to social chaos, at a time when the Japanese economy could hardly afford to deal with additional issues. The shift from emphasis on democratization to emphasis on economic growth was signaled by SCAP's **ban on the General Strike** of 1947.

As part of the "reverse course" the leadership clamped down on labor and began to side with management. The result was that many of the earlier purged personnel were rehabilitated as early as 1949 and a second purge—the "red purge"—began in 1950. It was an

した。政府の公職から1177人が共産主義者で
あるとの嫌疑で追放され、労働組合ではさら
に多くの人々が追放されました。レッド・パー
ジは直ちに民間の企業人、教員、工場労働者、
ジャーナリストにも及びました。米国でも同じ
ようなことが起き、ジョセフ・マッカーシー議
員の公聴会はその典型でした。

　驚くべきことに、占領期の非軍国主義化政
策も見直しの対象となりました。米国政府は、
ソ連から中国へと拡張する共産主義の勢力を
憂慮し始め、正規の警察を補完する15万人の
準軍事部隊を組織する権限をGHQに与えた
のです。マッカーサーは戦時中、米軍指揮官と
して太平洋の島々で日本軍と戦ったため、個
人的にはそのような部隊をつくることにため
らいがありました。

🔖 下山事件

　1949年7月、国鉄初代総裁・下山定則（しもやまさだのり）が、通勤中に立ち寄った三越本店
から、公用車を待たせたまま失踪し、翌日常磐線の線路上で轢死体となって、
発見されました。

　事件の真相はいまだに解明されていませんが、事件の背景としてさまざ
まな世情が挙げられます。

　1948年12月に出された「経済安定9原則」は1948年3月にドッジライ
ンとして実施されました。ドッジラインは財政金融引き締め政策で、インフ
レの抑制と輸出振興を目的としました。為替レートは1ドル＝360円の単
一レートに設定されました。財政引き締めのため、全公務員で28万人、国
鉄だけでも10万人もの人員整理を行いました。そのようななか、労働組合
や共産党が勢力を拡大しました。

　一方、朝鮮半島では、38度線を境界に共産政権（北朝鮮）と親米政権（韓
国）が一触即発の状態にあり、中国では中共軍の勝利が決定的となっていま

attempt to remove 1,177 alleged Communists from positions of responsibility in government and even more alleged Communists within the labor movement. Quickly it spread to private businesses and to teachers, factory workers and journalists. Similar actions were occurring in the United States, as exemplified by the **hearings** brought about by Sen. Joseph McCarthy.

Surprisingly enough, the demilitarization policy of the Occupation also came under **reconsideration**. As the American government began to worry about the strength of Communism extending from the Soviet Union into China, it authorized SCAP to create a Japanese **paramilitary force** of 150,000 members to act as a supplement to the regular police. MacArthur had led American troops against the Japanese military from island to island in the Pacific during the war, so he was personally hesitant to implement such a force.

した。そこで米国は日本を「反共の防波堤」と位置づけました。

そのような状況で起こった下山事件について、作家の松本清張は『日本の黒い霧』で米軍防諜報部隊（CIC）の関与説を描きました。ほかにも、人員整理の責任者として心身ともに疲れ果てていた下山総裁の自殺説もありました。「下山事件」は、その後立て続けに起きた「三鷹事件」（無人列車暴走事件）、「松川事件」（レール外しによる列車転覆事件）とともに国鉄の戦後3大ミステリーとされています。

松川事件。折り重なるように転覆した車両（1949年8月）

しかし、1950年6月25日に北朝鮮が韓国に侵攻すると、マッカーサーも自衛軍を認めるほかなくなりました。その年の夏には、米軍部隊が日本から朝鮮半島に飛び立ちました。その米軍の代わりとして、マッカーサーは日本政府に対し、「国内の治安」維持のために7万5000人からなる警察予備隊の招集を命じました。しかし新たな「警察」は、ライフル、マシンガン、迫撃砲、戦車で武装し、米国人の軍事顧問がついていました。ある人は、それは「小さな米軍」のようだったと記しています。

日本は陸海空軍を保持しないと新憲法第9条で謳ったことを考えると、日本人はそのような軍隊をどのように正当化したのでしょうか。まず、武力が「戦争を引き起こす可能性」がな

🌀 米国のマッカーシズム

　米国人の視点から見れば、1949年は冷戦期における最も無情な1年でした。ソ連が原爆を開発し、中国では共産主義政権が誕生しました。そして1950年には、科学者が米国の原爆に関する機密をソ連に売り渡したとして逮捕されました。こうした状況から米国人は、国内の共産主義者がスパイや国家反逆者の支援を受けているという疑いを持ち始めました。

　当時名が知れていなかった、ジョセフ・マッカーシーという共和党の上院議員は、選挙での落選を恐れ、売名目的で、米国には共産主義のスパイが大勢いると公言しました。1950年2月、彼は政府が共産主義に対して強い態度で臨んでいないと演説しました。1枚の紙を振りかざし「これは、国務長官が共産党員と認めている205人のリストだ。彼らは今も国務省で働き、政策を決定している！」と言い放ちました。

　しかし、実際には、そのようなリストは存在しなかったのです。マッカーシーはそのような告発を続け、知名度を拡大していきました。彼は証拠もでっちあげ、「スパイと思われる人」の人数も地位もころころと変えましたが、米国はわが意を得たりとばかりに彼の嘘に耳を傾けました。

But after North Korea invaded South Korea on June 25, 1950, MacArthur had little other choice than to do authorize a self-defense force. American troops left Japan for the **Korean peninsula** in the summer of that year. To replace them, MacArthur ordered the Japanese government to assemble a **National Police Reserve** of 75,000 men, to maintain "domestic tranquility." The new "police," however, were armed with rifles, machine guns, mortars, **artillery tanks** and American advisers. As one observer noted, they looked like a "little American army."

How were the Japanese to justify such a military force given the declaration of Article 9 of their new constitution, which stated that Japan would never maintain land, sea or air forces? First, it was held that Article 9

ジョセフ・マッカーシー
(1908–1957)

　他者を共産主義者と中傷する彼のやり方は「マッカーシズム」として知られるようになり、その結果、数千人が公職から追放されました。たとえば影響力のある下院非米活動調査委員会（HUAC）は、あらゆる分野の人々にワシントンでの証言を求め、喚問された人が反論すると「共産主義シンパ」の烙印を押し、職を失わせることもしばしばでした。自らの職と名声を守るために、他者を「共産主義思想に染まった者」と名指しで糾弾する人もいました。

　特にラジオ、娯楽映画、テレビでは、共産主義を喚起させると「ブラックリスト」に挙げられて仕事口がなくなりました。マッカーシーの影響は、彼が1954年に国防総省のスパイを告発しようとして失敗するまで、根強く続きました。その年の末、彼を支持する者は皆無となり、騒動にも終止符が打たれました。当時の大統領で同じ共和党のドワイト・アイゼンハワーは、「マッカーシズムは過去のものになった」と宣言しました。

ければ、第9条はそれを保持することを禁止していない、と考えました。次に、日本の政治指導者は、いかなる国家も武力によって防衛する権利を持つとする**国連憲章**に合致する「**自衛力**」を持つだけだ、として正当化しました。警察予備隊が**自衛隊**という名称に変わっても、それから半世紀以上、この軍事力が合憲か否かという議論が続いたのです。

東京裁判

　正式には**極東国際軍事裁判**として知られる東京裁判は、戦時中の政府および軍部の指導者を起訴し、1946年5月3日に開廷、1948年11月12日に閉廷しました。被告人の多くは、残虐行為を指揮した「B級戦犯」、もしくは比較的軽微な残虐行為や捕虜虐待を行った「C級戦犯」でした。それに加えて28人が、アジア・太平洋での戦争を計画・遂行した「A級戦犯」として起訴されました。裁判の結果、28人のうち25人が**有罪**となりました。これらのうち、東条英機元首相を含む7人が**絞首台**に送られました。**死刑**は、1948年12月23日に執行されました。18人は長期刑を言い渡されました。

東京裁判開廷（1946年5月3日）

did not prohibit such forces as long as they did not possess what could be called "war potential." Subsequently, Japanese leaders justified these forces as possessing only "**defensive capability**," which is in accord with the **United Nations Charter provision** that every nation has a right to defend itself militarily. The debate over whether this military force was constitutional would continue for over a half century after it was renamed the **Self Defense Forces**.

The Tokyo War Crimes Trial

Formally known as the **International Military Tribunal for the Far East**, the Tokyo War Crimes Trial brought charges against wartime government and military leaders of Japan, opening on May 3, 1946, and closing on November 12, 1948. Most of the accused were "Class B" criminals, accused of commanding their troops to commit atrocities, or "Class C" criminals, accused of committing comparatively minor atrocities or mistreating prisoners of war. In addition, 28 men were brought to trial as "Class A" criminals, accused of planning and waging Japan's aggression across Asia and the Pacific. At the end of the trials, 25 of the original 28 were **found guilty**. Of these, seven men, including former Prime Minister Tojo Hideki, were sent to the **gallows**. **Death sentences** were carried out on December 23, 1948. Eighteen of the men received extended prison sentences.

当時の日本国民が裁判について知ることができたのは、必然的に三つのことに限られました。第1に、日本国民は、日本軍による1937年の**南京大虐殺**をはじめとする中国と東南アジアにおける旧日本軍の残虐行為について初めて知りました。第2に、7人が絞首刑に処せられたことを知りました。第3に、天皇は出廷をまったく命ぜられなかったと聞きました。

勝利者の裁き?

裁判開始当初から、この裁判が合法か否か、という疑問が提起されました。この裁判は違法であると長年主張してきた人々は、裁判は「勝者の裁き」であり、**法的な報復**だったと批判してきました。彼らの見解はいくつかの前提に基づいています。第1に、裁判官に、他国の国民、つまり連合国による行為については**裁判権**を与えられなかった点です。例えば、二つの都市へ原爆を投下したトルーマン大統領を起訴すべきだと考える裁判官もいたのです。第2に、戦争遂行への関与だけでは、一般に世界で合意されたいかなる国際慣習においても戦争犯罪と規定されてこなかった点です。それがなぜ、この訴訟では戦争犯罪が裁判にかけられるものと見なされたのでしょうか。

これとは反対に、日本が海外での**侵略**や残虐行為の責任を十分に認めなかったことを指

What the Japanese public learned about the trial at that time was essentially limited to three things. First, they learned for the first time about the **massacre of Nanjing** in 1937 and other atrocities committed by the Japanese military in China and Southeast Asia. Second, they were informed that seven of the accused had been hanged. Third, they heard that the emperor had not been summoned before the court at all.

Victor's Justice?

From the beginning of the trials, the question has been raised as to whether the trials were legal. Those who have claimed through the years that the trials were illegal have condemned the trials as "victor's justice," a **legal cover for retaliation**. Their position rests of several premises. First, the judges were not given **jurisdiction** over acts committed by other nationals, meaning over the Allied Powers. One judge, for example, wanted to bring charges against President Truman for dropping atomic bombs on two Japanese cities. Second, merely participating in the waging of war had not been defined as a war crime in any of the conventions agreed upon by the world at large. Why was that to be considered a war crime in the immediate case before the court?

On the opposite side of the argument, some critics have pointed to Japan's failure to own up adequately to

摘した論者もいました。このような見解を持つ人たちが注目した点は、日本がドイツと異なり、戦争裁判を自発的に行わなかったということでした。おそらく当時の日本は、征服者が押し付けた裁判を受け入れざるを得なかったのですが、裁判にかけられた指導者たちは、天皇もしくは日本国民全体の単なるスケープゴートだった、という見方もありました。しかし裁判以来、大きな問題は残されたままです。なぜ天皇の責任は問われなかったのでしょうか。

天皇は軍部に利用されただけで、軍部の行為を止める実権はなかったと一貫して主張している人もいます。しかし、開戦を決定し、戦争をいかに進めるかを決定した御前会議に、天皇が直接関わっていたのは明らかでした。これを理由に、連合国のなかには天皇の名において行われた侵略行為の謀議、残虐行為の容疑で、天皇を起訴することを望んだ国もありました。

例えば、100万人以上の非戦闘員の犠牲者を出し、戦時中に壊滅的な打撃を被ったフィ

パール判事

　東京裁判でＡ級戦犯の罪に問われていた25人全員について、ただ一人無罪を主張した裁判官がいました。インド代表のパール判事です。彼が法廷に提出した意見書は「日本無罪論」と呼ばれ、日本の戦争責任を否定する人たちによって都合よく取り上げられていました。

　しかし、パール判事は米国の原爆投下など「勝者の戦争犯罪」を扱わない裁判のあり方そのものを批判し、侵略戦争を違法とする国際法はまだ存在しないとして、東京裁判の法理を否定したのです。以下は、後にパール判事

its responsibility for **aggression** and atrocities abroad. Of interest to those who hold this view is the fact that, unlike Germany, Japan did not conduct war trials on its own initiative. Perhaps Japanese at the time accepted the justice imposed by the **conquerors** as unavoidable, but some saw the leaders on trial as mere scapegoats—for the emperor, or for the Japanese people as a whole. But since the trials, a major issue has remained: Why wasn't the emperor charged?

Some have continually claimed that the emperor was merely used by the military and that he had no real power to prevent their actions. But it is evident that the emperor was directly involved in the **imperial conferences** where the decision to go to war and the decisions on how to pursue the war were made. Because of this, some Allies wanted to prosecute him for conspiring to commit aggression and allowing atrocities to be committed in his name.

The Philippines, for example, had lost more than one million **non-combatants** and suffered tremendous

が話したといわれている言葉です。

「私は日本の同情者として、また反対者として判決したのではありません。事実を事実と認め、自分の信ずる正しい法を適用したまでです」

「あの戦争裁判で、私は日本に道義的責任はあっても、法律的に責任がないという結論を下しました。法は、その適用すべき対象をあれこれと選ぶことはできないのです」

リピンは、裕仁には明白な戦争責任があり、裁判にかけられるべきだと主張しました。また、米国と英国は、3万6000人近く──全捕虜の4分の1以上──が捕虜収容所で死にました。生還した捕虜や遺族は、何十年も日本人に対して激しい怒りを抱いています。40年後に裕仁が死の床にあったとき、英国のタブロイド紙『ザ・サン』は、「死にゆく裕仁天皇について残念に思う理由が二つある。1）裕仁がかくも長く生きたこと、2）彼が今世紀の最も卑劣な犯罪を罰せられることなく死んでいくこと……死ねば、彼のための特別席が必ずや地獄に用意されているだろう」と論じました。

　しかし、ワシントンの政策立案者のなかのいわゆる「親日派」は、いかなる方法であれ、天皇を罰することは日本国民の痛烈な反感を招きかねない、と主張しました。最終的にその主張を通した「親日派」は、皇室制度がGHQによって立憲君主制に転換されれば、国家の社会構造を維持し、官僚機構との協力体制を築くことで、天皇を国家の安定に利用できると論じたのです。天皇という中心的存在がいなくなれば国が混乱をきたすと恐れる者もいました。この見解が主流となり、天皇が戦時の決定で重要な役割を果たしていたとしても、ほかの点への考慮から天皇の起訴は回避されました。戦後日本の指導者とGHQは、様々な動機から、この結末を導くために力を尽くしたのです。

damage during the war and they felt that Hirohito was clearly responsible and should be tried. Nearly 36,000 British and American prisoners of war—more than a fourth of all captured soldiers—had died in **captivity**. Survivors and families of the deceased would harbor intense anger against the Japanese for decades. When Hirohito was on his deathbed over four decades later, the British tabloid *The Sun* would write, "There are two reasons to be sorry about Emperor Hirohito being on his deathbed: 1) The fact that Hirohito lived this long, and 2) The fact that he will die without being punished for the most despicable crimes of this century.... When he dies, there will definitely be a special seat reserved for him in hell."

However, the so-called "**Japan crowd**" among American planners in Washington argued that an attempt to punish the emperor in any way could incite a severe reaction from Japanese citizenry. The "Japan crowd," ultimately the successful side, argued that if the **imperial institution** were converted by SCAP into a **constitutional monarchy**, the emperor could be used to stabilize the nation by holding together the social fabric of the nation and by guaranteeing the cooperation of the bureaucracy. Without the emperor as a central figure, some feared, the nation could fall into chaos. This view prevailed, so although the emperor was considered to have taken an active role in wartime decisions, other considerations prevented him from being put on trial. Both the postwar Japanese leaders and SCAP, with different motives, worked toward this end.

朝鮮戦争の衝撃

　朝鮮半島で勃発した悲劇的な戦争は、日本に多大な恩恵をもたらしました。日本は1950年の春に深刻な**不況**に直面していましたが、すぐに米軍の**軍需品**を調達するよう求められました。1951年から53年にかけて調達額は20億ドルに上り、輸出総額の約60％を占めました。生産は増大し、製造業は敗戦以来初めて

朝鮮戦争の特需兵器生産に励む女子工員（1950年）

利益を出し、新たな工場や設備への投資も急増しました。日本経済に限っていえば、当時の吉田茂首相の言葉通り、朝鮮戦争は「天佑神助」でした。

　戦争は、日本と朝鮮半島の二つの政府との関係に長期的な悪影響を及ぼすことになりました。日本はかつて朝鮮半島を植民地として統治し、その住人に日本産業に従事させ、独自の文化を捨てさせました。そして日本は朝鮮戦争で、米国による朝鮮半島爆撃の拠点として、また米軍配置の**中継基地**としての役割を果たしたのです。

吉田茂

　吉田茂ほど、日本を変えようとした人物はいません。彼は戦前、外交官としてロンドン、

Impact of the Korean Conflict

The tragic war that broke out on the Korean peninsula was a great **boon** to Japan. Faced with a deepening
depression in the spring of 1950, Japan was immediately called on to fill American **military procurement**
orders. In the years 1951–1953, these procurements
amounted to two billion dollars, approximately 60% of
all of Japan's exports. Production rose, manufacturers
began to show profits for the first time since the surrender and there was a surge of investment in new plants
and equipment. As far as the Japanese economy was
concerned, the Korean War was, in the words of Yoshida
Shigeru, "a gift of the gods."

The war would have long-term repercussions in relations between Japan and the governments of the peninsula. Japan had ruled the peninsula as a colony, forcing
its residents to serve in Japan's industries and shed
Korean cultural identity. Then in the Korean War, Japan
served as a base for American bombing raids on the peninsula and as a **staging ground** for the deployment of
U.S. troops.

Yoshida Shigeru

Perhaps no one personified that will to change Japan as
much as Yoshida Shigeru, who had served as a prewar

中国に赴任しましたが、戦時中には退官して一般人となっていました。戦後、その「国際派」としての経歴がGHQに認められ、外相を短期間務めた後、1949年に67歳で首相に就任しました。

1930年代と1940年代初頭はそれまでの民主主義、資本主義への道のりから短期間ながら外れ、軍国主義の妨害を受けていたのだ、と吉田は確信していました。占領当局が全力を挙げて取り組むべきは、軍国主義とその支持者を一掃し、日本が国際社会の一員となるべく経済を活性化させて日本を**再建**することだ、と彼は主張しました。左翼と労働組合には強固な姿勢を堅持し、米国人には断固たる姿勢で臨みました。特に、独立し、経済的に繁栄し、政治的に安定した日本を築くカギは、日本の官僚、政治家、経済界の指導者に改革の遂行

を任せることだとの考えから、GHQに疎まれもしました。追放されていた政治家が復権したことで吉田は失脚しましたが、その影響力は、彼が育てた政治家たち、――「吉田学校」――1980年代まで日本を率いた池田勇人、佐藤栄作、大平正芳、中曾根康弘らを通じて残りました。

吉田茂（1878–1967）

diplomat in London and China, but who had sat out the war years as an ordinary citizen. His record as an "internationalist" helped him win favor with SCAP after the war and he was encouraged to serve as foreign minister briefly before he took on the duties of prime minister in 1949 at the age of 67.

Yoshida was convinced that the 1930s and early 1940s were a short-term detour from the earlier path of democracy and capitalism, interrupted by the militarists. He contended that all the Occupation needed to do was to expel the militarists and their supporters, stimulate the economy and help **reestablish** Japan as a participating member in the international community. Tough with the Left and the trade unions, he was stubborn with the Americans. In particular, he rankled SCAP with his view that the key to creating an independent, economically prosperous and politically stable Japan was to leave implementation up to Japanese bureaucrats, politicians and business leaders. Although he would fall from power with the return of purged politicians, his influence continued through the politicians he groomed—the so-called "Yoshida school" (*Yoshida gakko*)—who were to lead Japan into the 1980s: Ikeda Hayato, Sato Eisaku, Ohira Masayoshi, and Nakasone Yasuhiro.

講和条約

　1950年までに、いくつかの要素が、当初の計画より長引いていた占領の終結決定に結びつきました。マッカーサー自身、3年だけという当初の計画に沿って、1947年春の占領終結を要請していました。彼は、連合国は、日本がミズーリ船艦上で調印した「**降伏**」に代わる正式な講和条約を日本と締結すべきだと提言していました。朝鮮戦争の勃発により、トルーマン大統領はマッカーサーを韓国駐留**国連軍**の指揮官に任命しました。その後、マッカーサーは軍事政策をめぐってトルーマンと公然と対立しました。トルーマンは直ちに、韓国での**軍指揮権**と、日本を統治していた連合国軍最高司令官の職務を剥奪しました。

　マッカーサーに代わり、後に国務長官とな

「老兵は死なず、ただ消え去るのみ」

　マッカーサーはGHQの総司令官としての任にあった1948年、米国の大統領選挙に出馬する旨の声明を出しました。この声明に一番敏感に反応したのは日本人でした。街には「マ元帥を大統領に」という垂れ幕が掲げられ、新聞には彼を後押しする記事が載せられました。彼は、「日本軍兵士の引き揚げに尽力してくれている」と日本国民に人気があったのです。しかし、マッカーサーは共和党の人統領候補者選出で支持を得られませんでした。結局、本選では、民主党の現職大統領のトルーマンが再選を果たしました。
　1950年、金日成が率いる北朝鮮軍が韓国に侵攻することによって勃発し

Peace Treaty

By 1950 several factors led to a decision to bring an end to the Occupation, which had already lasted far longer than planned. MacArthur himself had called for an end to the Occupation in the spring of 1947—in line with the original plan for Occupation to continue just three years. He suggested that it was time for the Allied Powers to conclude a formal peace treaty with Japan that would replace the formal "**surrender**" that Japan had signed on the *USS Missouri*. When the Korean War broke out, President Truman appointed MacArthur to serve as commander of the **UN forces** in Korea. MacArthur later publicly disagreed with Truman over matters of military policy. Truman immediately relieved him of both his **military command** in Korea and his position as the Supreme Commander of Allied Powers which governed Japan.

Instead of MacArthur, it would be John Foster

た朝鮮戦争は、一進一退の戦況となります。マッカーサーは朝鮮戦争でも指揮を執りました。しかし、彼が戦況打開のために空爆と核攻撃の必要性を説くとトルーマンと対立し、更迭されました。

　マッカーサーの引退、帰国の日には、20万人の日本人と多くの報道陣がつめかけ、彼を見送りました。帰国後、彼は退任に際しての演説で、次の有名な言葉を残しています。

　　「老兵は死なず、ただ消え去るのみ
　　（Old soldiers never die, they just fade away）」

るジョン・フォスター・ダレスが米国の各同盟国と協議を行い、日本と講和条約の交渉を行いました。数多くの検討課題があり、また両国とも優先問題を抱えていました。日本の侵略行為により最も損害を被った東南アジア諸国は、莫大な**賠償**を日本に求めていました。英国は自国のアジア市場の権益を守るため、日本の将来の輸出に制限を加えるよう求めました。第1次世界大戦後のドイツの**怨恨**がナチスの台頭と第2次世界大戦を引き起こしたことから、日本の怨恨が同様の事態を引き起こさないよう寛大な対処を求める国々もありました。

　日本国内では、西側諸国、共産主義世界のどちらとも手を組まずに中立を保ち、**再軍備**を拒否し、日本領土内の米軍駐留を認めないよう求める声があがりました。吉田首相自身は、条約に将来の日本の政治・経済活動への規制を一切設けないようにすべく交渉にあたりました。彼は中立的立場を排し、**対米協調路線**を採用しました。彼はまた、**米軍駐留**を受け入れる以外に選択の余地はほとんどないと判断しました。しかしダレスが、地上軍30万人による再軍備を提案すると、吉田は応じられないとする様々な理由を示しました。第1に日本の経済力ではそのような軍隊を維持できないこと、第2に苦い戦争を経験した日本国民が容認しないこと、第3に憲法第9条がそのような軍隊の設立を禁じていること、第4にほかのアジア諸国がそのような考えを受け入れないだろう、というものでした。

Dulles, later Secretary of State, who would negotiate the peace treaty with Japan through consultation with all of America's allies during the war. There were many issues to take into account, and each nation had its own priorities. The nations of Southeast Asia that had suffered the most from Japanese aggression expected heavy **reparations** from Japan. Great Britain wanted to limit Japan's future export potential in order to protect British markets in Asia. Others called for lenience in order to prevent resentment in Japan that might parallel German **resentment** at the end of World War I which led to the rise of the Nazis and World War II.

Within Japan, there were calls for Japan to remain neutral, siding with neither the West nor the Communist world, to reject **rearmament** and to prohibit U.S. forces from remaining on Japanese soil. Prime Minister Yoshida himself bargained for a treaty that would place no restrictions on the economic or political future of Japan. He rejected calls for neutrality and instead favored an **alignment with the U.S.** He was also convinced that Japan had little choice other than to allow the **stationing of U.S. troops** in Japan. But when Dulles proposed that Japan plan to rearm with a ground force of 300,000 men, Yoshida produced a list of reasons why that could not be carried out. First, Japan could not afford such a force. Second, the Japanese public, sick of wartime military, would not tolerate such a force. Third, Article 9 banned the formation of such a force. Fourth, the other Asian nations would reject such an idea.

街にあふれる講和気分
（1951年9月3日）

　数カ月に及ぶ交渉の末、日本、米国のほか、日本のかつての敵国50カ国がサンフランシスコに集まり、講和会議が開かれました。1951年9月8日、同会議は講和条約に正式に調印し、戦争状態は最終的に終結しました。重大なことに、ソ連は議事進行中に**退席し**、**正統政権**が中華民国と中華人民共和国のどちらかということに国際的合意が得られなかった中国は会議に招かれませんでした。その結果、日本は近隣の2大国と正式な講和を結ぶことができなかったのです。

　大方の予想通り、合意内容は日本に寛容なものでした。続いていた戦争状態の終結、条約締結から90日以内の占領軍撤退、日本の主権回復、日本の自衛権が承認されました。そのなかでも重要だったのは、日本の経済や貿易を制限する条項が皆無だったことです。

　講和条約が締結されて数時間のうちに、日米両政府の代表は**日米安全保障条約**に調印しました。これは、米軍を日本国内に**無期限に**駐留することを認める条約です。このことは、半世紀以上に渡って日本の国内外で議論を巻き起こしています。日本は、駐日米軍の費用の一部を負担することになっています。また、日本の防衛は、政権交代のたびに変わる米国の政策に左右されることになります。米国は日本政府との協議も事前通告の義務もなく、日本国内の基地から世界のどこへでも軍を派遣できます。結果的に、その軍事行動は日本を危険

After months of negotiations between the various parties involved, Japan, the United States and 50 of Japan's other former enemies gathered in San Francisco for a formal peace conference. On September 8, 1951, a formal peace conference signed the treaty bringing the state of war to a final end. Significantly, the Soviet Union **walked out** of the proceedings and China was not invited because of international disagreement over whether the **legitimate government** was located in Beijing or Taipei. This left Japan without a formal declaration ending war status with its two largest neighbors.

By most estimates, the terms of the settlement were generous to Japan. The still-remaining state of war was terminated, occupation personnel would be withdrawn within 90 days of the effect of the treaty, Japan received its sovereignty back and Japan's right to defend itself was delineated. Of great importance was the provision that no limits were to be placed on Japan's economy or trade.

Within hours, representatives of both governments signed the **United States–Japan Security Treaty**, a document which would permit the U.S. to station troops in Japan **indefinitely**. The granting of this permission has, for over a half-century, provoked debate within Japan and abroad. Japan is obliged to defray some of the expenses for the troops that are stationed in Japan. It subordinates Japan's defense needs to U.S. policy, which changes from administration to administration. The U.S. is free to dispatch the troops stationed in Japan anywhere in the world without consulting with or even notifying Japanese authorities. As a result, such

にさらすこともあるのです。米国が、自国の利
益にのみ合致する紛争に日本を引きずり込む
軍事行動を、駐日基地から開始するかもしれ
ません——それは日本の国益に反するかもし
れないのです。一方、米国は日本の防衛力の主
軸になりました。米国の**核の庇護**のもと、日本
はGNPのわずか1%を防衛費に充て、残りを
民間企業経営、個人消費や貯蓄にまわすこと
ができたのです。

　講和条約と安全保障条約が各国に批准さ
れ、発効したのは1952年4月28日です。その
結果、占領は終結し、冷戦時代に日本は西側陣
営と足並みを揃え、経済援助と軍事的保護を
確かなものとしました。公式の平和条約では
ないものの、日ソ共同宣言により1956年には
日本とソ連の国交が回復しました。同年には、
日本の国連加盟が承認されました。

占領期の映画・文芸作品

　戦時中日本の軍国主義政府は文化面で厳し
い**検閲**を行いましたが、占領期のGHQによ
る検閲も変わらず厳しいものでした。例えば
GHQ批判と原爆批判は占領が終結するまで
タブーでした。しかし、飢餓（吉村公山郎監督
『象を喰った連中』1947年）、売春（溝口健二

actions may place Japan at risk. The U.S. might launch a military action from Japan that would drag Japan into a conflict that served only U.S. interests—and might actually be against Japan's interests. On the other hand, the U.S. became the mainstay of Japan's defense. Under the American **nuclear umbrella**, Japan would end up spending only 1% of its GNP on its own defense, leaving more of the nation's resources to **private enterprise**, personal consumption and individual savings.

The peace and security treaties were ratified by the respective governments and went into effect on April 28, 1952. As a result, the Occupation ended, the nation stood with the West in the Cold War era and Japan was assured of economic assistance and military protection. Although not a formal peace treaty, the Soviet–Japanese Joint Declaration reestablished diplomatic relations between the two countries in 1956. In that same year Japan was granted membership in the United Nations.

Postwar Literature

While the Japanese military government had strictly **censored** cultural expression during the war, SCAP had been no less strict during the Occupation. Criticism of SCAP and the nuclear bombings, for example, were taboo until the Occupation came to an end, but portrayals of hunger (Yoshimura's *The Fellows Who Ate the*

監督『赤線地帯』1948年）、歴史上の女性の不遇（溝口健二監督『西鶴一代女』1952年）、暗躍するヤクザ（黒澤明監督『酔いどれ天使』1948年）、自己の行動に対する個人の責任（黒澤明監督『野良犬』1949年）といったテーマで、荒廃した世界が鮮明に描き出されました。竹山道雄は1948年に『ビルマの竪琴』を著し、終戦後も出征地ビルマに残って仏教の僧侶となり、死んだ戦友の**遺骨**を集める道を選ぶ元日本兵、水島を描きました。竹山の作品は、戦争の悲劇を仏僧の視点から描こうとしたものでした。

　1949年には、戦うために前線に赴いた大学生たちの手紙や日記を集めた『きけわだつみのこえ——日本戦没学生の手記——』が出版され、ベストセラーとなりました。「わだつみ」とは日本神話に登場する海の神であり、太平洋に散った学生たちのことでした。進歩的な知識人によって文書75点が編纂されました。文学的感覚にあふれ、思索に満ちた戦争犠牲者たちの声を、無駄にされた命、悲劇的な死を伝える作品に仕上げたのです。書き手は国のために死ぬ使命を受け入れながらも生への渇望を訴えており、反戦を訴える書物となっています。出版時期も極めて重要です。この書物は、第2次世界大戦の悲劇を振り返るものですが、朝鮮戦争が勃発し、米国が日本に再軍備を求め、初期の平和運動が高まっていた時期に出版されたのです。

Elephant, 1947), prostitution (Mizoguchi's *Women of the Night*, 1948), the tragic fate of women in history (Mizoguchi's *The Life of Oharu*, 1952), the spread of gangsters (Kurosawa's *Drunken Angel*, 1948) and the responsibility of individuals for their own actions (Kurosawa's *Stray Dog*, 1949) clearly portrayed a world in ruins. Takeyama Michio published *Harp of Burma* in 1948, in which he portrayed a Japanese former soldier named Mizushima who at war's end did not return to Japan but rather chose to stay in Burma as a Buddhist priest in order to collect the **remains** of his countrymen who had died there. Takeyama's work of fiction attempted to deal with the tragedy of war from a Buddhist point of view.

In 1949, letters and diaries of university students who had gone off to fight at the front were published under the title *Listen! The Voices of the Ocean (Kike wadatsumi no koe)* and the volume became a bestseller. The term *wadatsumi* referred to the god of the sea and the students who had died in the Pacific Ocean. The collection of some 75 entries was edited by a group of progressive intellectuals. They transformed the voices of literate, reflective war casualties into a work that conveyed a sense of lives wasted and tragic loss. While accepting the mission of dying for their country, the writers showed a hunger for life, making the volume a statement against war. The timing of the publication was also highly significant. While it looked backward to the tragedy of World War II, it appeared at the time of the outbreak of the Korean War, a time when the U.S. was trying to get Japan to rearm itself and when the

映画『二十四の瞳』のポスター（1954年）

占領軍の撤退に続き、様々な角度から戦時中の問題を描いた映画が制作されました。米軍撤退の翌年には、日本軍と同様に米軍にも非理があると批判した小林正樹監督の『壁あつき部屋』（1953年）が制作されました。この作品は戦犯とされた人物数人も単なるスケープゴートとして取り上げました。木下恵介監督の『二十四の瞳』（1954年）は、いかなる強い意志も歴史の流れに逆らえない虚しさを抒情的に描きました。1952年に出版された大岡昇平の小説『野火』を原作とした市川崑監督の同名映画（1959年）は、フィリピン・レイテ島を舞台に飢餓に追いつめられた日本兵のカニバリズムを描きました。

戦後初期の映画作品のなかで最も象徴的だったのは、黒澤明監督の『羅生門』（1950年）でしょう。『羅生門』では、一つの出来事をまったく違う視点から描くことで、人が拠って立つ事実などいかにはかないものか、ということを示しました。実際、この世のあらゆることは、ものの見方によって変わってしまうのです。

復興への道のり

1952年の占領終了に続く政治情勢においては、新たな政党の形成と、政党間の連携再編が

early peace movement was taking form.

Following the departure of the American Occupation, filmmakers took up the issues of wartime in diverse ways. The year immediately following the departure of the Americans, Kobayashi Masaki's *Room with Thick Walls*, 1953, charged the Americans as equals of the Japanese army when it came to committing atrocities. The film also portrayed several of the convicted war criminals as mere scapegoats. Kinoshita Keisuke's *Twenty-four Eyes*, 1954, emphasized with considerable sentimentality that sometimes, even with the best of intentions at heart, it is impossible to stand against the flow of historical events. Ichikawa Kon's 1959 movie based on Ooka Shohei's 1952 novel *Fires on the Plain*, showed Japanese troops reduced to cannibalism during the battle of Leyte.

Perhaps the most symbolic of all the immediate postwar films was Kurosawa Akira's *Rashomon*, 1950, because with its multiple perspectives it showed that there is little that one can depend on as factual. Virtually everything depends upon one's point of view.

Hard Work of Recovery

The political scene following the end of the Occupation in 1952 featured the formation of new political parties

顕著でした。1955年には自由民主党と日本社会党が結成されます。この両者の関係は実質的に二大政党制を形成するもので、「55年体制」として知られるようになりました。**保守勢力**の自民党が国会の3分の2、**革新勢力**の社会党が3分の1の議席を持っていました。自民党主導のこのシステム——自民党については、複数の論者が自由でも民主的でもなく、実質的に政党とはいえないと評していました——は、細川護熙が初めて非自民党選出の首相になるまで38年間も続きました。自民党は、5、6派ほどの派閥集合体となって活動し、折衷主義的政策を展開し、党の指揮に関しては派閥同士で調整を図り、交代で首相を輩出しました。

　自民党は、農家に対する**農産物補助金**の確約、中小企業主への支援制度の拡大、工場労働者の労働条件の改善や給与引き上げなどによって成功しました。首相のポストを堅守し、官僚との長期的連携を築くこともできました。自民党の支持率は、1960年代中盤には40%に達しましたが、汚職が表面化した1970年代に25%に下落し、1970年代後半に33%まで持ち直しました。

and shifting alliances between those parties. In 1955 the Liberal Democratic Party (LDP) and the Japan Socialist Party (JSP) were formed. Their relationship would form an essentially **two-party political arrangement** that came to be known as the 1955 System. The **conservative** LDP managed a 2/3rds majority in the Diet with the **progressive** JSP holding the other 1/3rd of the seats. This system dominated by the LDP—which as more than one critic has noted was neither liberal nor democratic and was not actually a party—would dominate Japanese politics for the next 40 years, until Hosokawa Morihiro became the first non-LDP prime minister. The LDP acted as a gathering of a half-dozen factions, which advocated an eclectic set of policies, negotiated with other factions for control and rotated the role of the prime minister between themselves.

The LDP was successful because the factions reached out to diverse constituencies—guaranteeing **crop subsidies** to farmers, expanding welfare programs to small business owners, and improving working conditions and wages for factory workers. The party had a lock on the prime minister's post, and it was able to develop long-term relations with the bureaucracy. Popular support of the LDP would vary between a high of 40% in the mid-1960s to just over 25% during the scandals of the mid 1970s, but then rebound to 33% by the late 1970s.

高度経済成長

　1945年当時の壊滅状態や、日々の食卓を整えるにも長らく汲々としていたことを考えれば、終戦後10年を経ても日本のGNPが米国のわずか15分の1だったことは驚きに値しません。賃金はかろうじて戦前のピーク時のレベルに回復したばかりでした。日本経済がこれから飛躍するとの期待は、極めて楽観的に見えました。例えば、つい1955年まで労働力の41%は農業に集中しており、一方で西ドイツは18%、米国は9%、英国は4%でした。しかし、まさしくこの1955年から「高度経済成長」が始まったのです。

　最初に経済に拍車がかかったのは、米国が朝鮮半島に介入したときでした。1950年から1953年まで、日本は日本海の向こうで戦う米軍のために貢献しました。軍事行動に表立っ

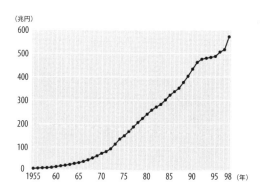

日本のGNPの推移
Gross National
Product

*内閣府データより

High-speed Growth

Judging from the devastation that Japan faced in 1945 and the prolonged struggle to simply keep food on the table day by day, it is no surprise that ten years later the GNP of the nation was still a mere 1/15th that of the United States. Wages by that time had just barely returned to the level of even the best of the prewar years. Any predictions that the Japanese economy was about to take off would have seemed excessively optimistic. As late as 1955, for example, 41% of Japan's labor force was working on farms, compared with 18% in West Germany, 9% in the U.S. and 4% in England. And yet, that is precisely what happened, and the year 1955 marked the beginning of "high-speed growth."

煙突からの排煙にかすむ尼崎市の工場地帯（1970年2月）

An initial spur to the economy had already occurred when America went to war in the Korean peninsula. From 1950 to 1953 Japan served as the base for U.S. forces fighting across the Sea of Japan. While obviously not involved militarily, Japan was economically deeply involved as a result of receiving two billion dollars in contracts for textiles, paper, lumber, steel and vehicles.

て関与はしなかったものの、米軍から20億ド
ルに及ぶ繊維、紙、木材、鉄鋼、輸送機の発注
を受けて経済的には深く関係していました。

この外部からの刺激による恩恵なくして、日
本が新たな工場や機械に投資できたとは思え
ません。また、限られた**埋蔵鉱物**や輸入した石
油をほかの**主幹産業**に充てることができたかど
うかも疑問です。まさに戦時調達による特需が
刺激となって、経済の産業部門が復活できたの
です。トヨタと日産はこの時期のトラック生産
から大きな資金力を得て、その後の平和な時代
における企業拡大の基盤を築きました。クボタ
は戦時調達による利益で、農機具、建設機具の
増産に乗り出しました。日本の産業は1955年
までに**完全な復興**へと歩み出したのです。

都市生活の変化

都市部は1950年代中盤までに**驚くべき成
長**を経験しました。戦時中、比較的安全だった
地方に疎開していた人々が戻り始めると、都
市部では住宅の建設ラッシュが始まりました。
かつて**平屋**があったところに、地方からの移
住者の住宅用にアパートが建設されました。
興味深いことに、それらの新たな住宅は、戦前
の数世代に渡る大家族用ではなく、**核家族**の
ために設計されました。都市スタイルの理想
は「2DKのアパート」──二つの寝室、居間、

Without profits from this external stimulus it is doubtful whether Japan could have begun to invest in new factories and machinery. It is also doubtful whether it could have redirected the limited **coal reserves** and imported oil supplies toward the **key industries**. With the stimulus of quick profits from war orders, the industrial sector of the economy was able to make a resurgence. Toyota and Nissan won contracts for trucks which returned these enterprises to solvency and gave them a base to expand from during the following peacetime. Kubota later used its profits from procurements to increase production of farm and construction equipment. Hence by 1955 Japanese industry was at the point of **full recovery**.

Urban Life Transformed

Urban Japan experienced **staggering growth** by the mid-1950s. When those who had left the cities during wartime for the relative safety of the countryside began to return to the cities, they triggered a boom in housing construction. Where there had once been **single-story residences**, apartment buildings were constructed to provide housing for the migrants from the countryside. Significantly, such new housing was intended for **nuclear families**, not for the extended, multiple-generation families of the prewar era. The urban ideal

経済白書が「もはや戦後ではない」とうたった1956年、冷蔵庫、洗濯機、白黒テレビが「三種の神器」といわれ農家にも普及した（1956年9月）

台所——となり、**団地**が都会の景観にそびえるようになりました。

日々の生活のことしか考えられなかった時代からより良い暮らしを求める時代に移ったことを象徴しているのが、1955年に登場した新語「マイホーム主義」です。これは家電メーカーが希望に満ちた新しい家電製品、特に現代日本における「**三種の神器**」と呼ばれた洗濯機、冷蔵庫、白黒テレビを主婦に売るために用いられたコピーでした。

8年後の1966年には「新三種の神器」もしくは「三つのＣ」——カラーテレビ、クーラー、車（カー）——が喧伝されるようになっていました。

所得倍増計画

1960年、池田勇人首相は「国民所得倍増計画」を実施しました。その目的は、完全雇用と、国民総生産（GNP）と実質国民所得の倍増を1970年までに実現し、誰もが消費の「三種の神器」を持てるようにするというものでした。科学技術に集中的に投資し、国際貿易を拡大し、**急成長産業への税控除**と**特別融資**措置により、向こう10年での国の富の倍増を目指したのです。それまで政府が採った経済政策のすべてが実を結んだわけではないなかで、こ

became a "2DK apartment"—two bedrooms, dining room and kitchen—and huge **apartment complexes** (*danchi*) sprouted across the urban landscape.

Emblematic of the transition from sheer survival mode to a quest for a better life was the coining of the term "my-home-ism" (*mai-homu-shugi*) in about 1955. It was used by the electrical appliance industry to sell gleaming new home appliances to housewives, especially the "**three sacred treasures**" (*sanshu no jingi*) of modern Japan: the washing machine, refrigerator and black and white television.

Eight years later in 1966, the "new three sacred treasures" (*shin sanshu no jingi*) or "3Cs" were being promoted: color TV, air conditioner (called "cooler" in Japanese) and the car.

Income-Doubling Plan

In 1960 Prime Minister Ikeda Hayato adopted as an official policy his "Income-Doubling Plan." Its purpose was to achieve full employment and double both GNP and personal income by 1970, making the "sacred treasures" of consumerism obtainable. By investing heavily in science and technology, expanding international trade and giving **tax breaks** and **special loans** to **high-growth industries**, this plan intended to double the national wealth of the country in the following decade. Not all government-declared policies reach fruition, but this

の政策は成功しました。なにより**国民所得**は10年どころか、わずか7年で倍増したのです。

資本が工場、設備、技術開発に投下され、日本企業は、「メイド・イン・ジャパン」の品物の**安かろう、悪かろう**というイメージを払拭しようとしていました。企業は国際市場に参入し、日本のGNPは資本主義諸国のうち第5位になりました。1960年代を通じて、日本経済は毎年平均10%以上という驚異的な成長率を遂げました。1960年代末には、日本のモノとサービスの生産力は**資本主義諸国**のうち第2位となり、かつての統治者、米国に次ぐ地位にのし上がったのです。

この経済発展に直接関与したのが、1949年に発足した通商産業省であったことは**火を見るよりも明らか**です。通産省の官僚は輸出入を規制する権限を持ち、悪名高き「**行政指導**」によって産業の方向付けを行うとともに、高度成長に最大限貢献するとして政府が選んだ産業部門に、海外の技術や原料を積極的に導入しました。通産省の「要請」や「提案」は「命令」とみなされました。通産省が新たな工場設立や、特定産業へ低利貸付を認可する権限を有していたからです。通産省の官僚が当初優遇したのは**造船業と鉄鋼業**であり、その後、自動車産業、さらにハイテク産業となりました。

朝鮮戦争で特需の恩恵を受けたときと同様に、日本は1965年から1973年まで、ベトナム

one did. To top it off, **national income** doubled within just seven years, instead of ten.

Money was invested in plants, equipment and developing technology and Japanese companies were about to erase the image that anything "made in Japan" was **cheaply and poorly made**. Companies competed for international markets, raising Japan's GNP to the fifth largest of the capitalist economies. Through the 1960s the economy grew at a phenomenal average rate of more than 10% per year. By the end of the 1960s, Japan's production of goods and services brought it to second place in the **capitalist nations**—second only to that of its former ruler, the U.S.

The government's direct hand in economic development is **nowhere more visible** than in the Ministry of International Trade and Industry (MITI), formed in 1949. MITI officials were given the power to control import and export permits. They used notorious "**administrative guidance**" (*gyosei shido*) to direct industry, together with the positive reinforcement of funneling foreign technology and raw materials into industry sectors that the government selected as contributing the most to high-speed growth. "Requests" and "proposals" from MITI were considered "orders," for MITI had control over licensing of new plants and low-interest loans to specific industries. Among the early favorites of MITI officials were **shipbuilding** and steel, followed later by the automobile industry and even later by high-tech industries.

Just as it had benefited from procurement contracts during the Korean War, Japan benefited again between

戦争中の米軍による新たな特需で再び恩恵を受けました。1966年の1年だけで、米国は戦争に約50億ドルを費やし、その相当額が日本に流れました。

公害

東海道新幹線の車窓に映る富士山の景観が、いまだに見苦しい工場の**煙突**に邪魔されている、と海外からの観光客は少なからず口にします。しかし、1950年代後半から1960年代にかけて、実質的に国中の住宅地が深刻な公害に直面しました。1970年代まで、住民が街路でゴミをドラム缶に入れて燃やす光景が日常的に見られ、フィルター処理されない工場の煙突からは煙も出ていました。政府による規制はほとんどなく、企業は焼却するか排水路に流すという最も経済的な方法で廃棄物を処理しており、**有毒廃棄物**の処理にほとんど注意を払っていませんでした。

政府は国家の経済を強化するために産業を支援しましたが、その政策の負の側面として、汚染の影響を事実上無視してしまったことが挙げられます。最初に公害対策の**怠慢**が表面化したのは1953年のことで、熊本県の水俣湾周辺の住民が中毒性の病気に苦しむようになり、猫などのペットにも同じ症状が現れまし

1965 and 1973 from a new round of procurement orders from the U.S. military during the Vietnam War. In 1966 alone, the U.S. invested approximately five billion dollars in fighting the war, and an enormous portion of that flowed into Japan.

Industrial Pollution

More than one visitor from overseas has commented on the unpleasant factory **smokestacks** that still interrupt the view of Mt. Fuji seen from the Tokaido Shinkansen. But during the late 1950s and 1960s residents faced heavy pollution in virtually every neighborhood of the nation. Until the 1970s it was common to see local residents burning trash in tin containers along the streets, adding to the haze produced by unfiltered local factory smokestacks. With few restrictions imposed by the government, businesses took the most economical means of disposing of wastes by incinerating it or dumping it into waterways, paying little attention to what happened to **toxic waste** thereafter.

While the government supported industry as a means of strengthening the national economy, among the negative side effects of that policy was a virtual disregard for the impact of pollution. The earliest sign of this **negligence** came in 1953 when the people living along Minamata Bay in Kumamoto Prefecture began to suffer a paralytic disease that also affected pets like cats.

た。以前から住民は猫が奇妙な歩き方をして、足からガクッと倒れ、頭がおかしくなったように走り回って口から泡を吹くのを見ていました。鳥も止まり木から落ちたり、建物や木に衝突したりしていました。その後、健康な人が、手がひどく震えたり、思考障害を煩うようになりました。**麻痺**はまず口と手足に始まり、その後、視覚、運動、言語障害の症状が現れました。症状が悪化すると、身体の自由がきかなくなり、多くの人が寝たきりや、**意識不明**になりました。

　濃縮した**有機水銀**が脳細胞を破壊し、自律神経障害、感覚の麻痺、言語障害、ひどい痙攣などを引き起こしたのです。重度の場合は数週間で死に至ることもあり、緩やかに症状が進行することもありました。また妊婦が水銀を摂取すると、子どもはいわゆる先天性水俣病となりました。

　厚生省は1968年にようやく、新日本窒素肥料の水俣工場が水俣湾に廃棄した有機水銀がそれらの病気の原因であると認めました。湾に生息する魚が水銀を取り込み、その魚を食べた住民が中毒に冒されたのです。1961年までに87件の水銀中毒の症例が確認されました。企業と政府を訴えた被害者を支援する抗議運動も起こり、長く続いた裁判の結果、部分的な勝訴となりました。その過程で、日本人は初めて、いかなる犠牲を払ってでも経済発展を推し進める政策の危険性に気づいたのです。

Residents had seen cats walking strangely, falling over their own legs, going mad, running in circles and foaming at the mouth. Birds fell off their perches and flew into buildings and trees. Then, healthy humans found their hands trembling violently and their minds unable to think clearly. **Numbness** that began in the lips and limbs was followed by disturbances in vision, movement and speech. As symptoms grew worse, control over their bodies diminished and many became bedridden and fell into **unconsciousness**.

Concentrations of **organic mercury** destroyed human brain cells and lead to symptoms such as loss of coordination, lack of sensation, loss of speech and convulsions. In severe cases, the mercury could cause death within weeks, and in other cases it had a more gradual effect. Where pregnant women were exposed to mercury, their children were born with what became known as congenital Minamata disease.

It took until 1968 for the Welfare Department to determine that the cause of the disease was the mercury that the Japan Chisso Company factory was dumping into the bay. The mercury was taken in by the fish in the bay and the people who ate those fish suffered the consequences. By 1961 some 87 cases of mercury poisoning had been confirmed. Protestors began to rally behind the sufferers who sued the company and the government, winning a partial victory after many years in court. In the process, Japanese for the first time became broadly aware of the dangers that accompanied

水俣病で自由のきかない患者の手（1970年）

　水俣の汚染は社会への警鐘となったものの、ほとんど関心を得られませんでした。カドミウム汚染が、富山県神通川流域の住民に激しい苦痛をもたらしたのです。これは後に「イタイイタイ病」として知られるようになりました。四日市市（名古屋の近く）と川崎市（横浜の近く）は、スモッグと、**水棲生物**が絶滅するほどの水質汚染で知られるようになりました。漁場がカドミウムや水銀でひどく汚染された地域では、**魚介類が食用に適さなくなったため、**漁師が廃業に追い込まれました。被害者は抗議運動や裁判で補償を求めましたが、たいていの場合、汚染企業は責任逃れをし、調査を妨害しました。地方自治体や国の行政も比較的消極的なままでした。

　しかし1960年代後半になると、汚染被害者たちは全国に支援ネットワークを築き、ボイコットや座り込みを始めました。最終的に1967年、国会で包括的な**公害対策基本法**が可決され、住民運動による公害企業に対する多くの訴訟の基盤となりました。特に1971年から1973年の間に下された画期的な一連の判決は、被害者の補償を認め、公害防止措置を築く助けとなりました。その結果、その空は青空に戻らないまでも、鼻をつくような異臭や黄味がかったスモッグは消えました。

policies of economic development at all costs.

The pollution at Minamata served as a warning, but one that was mostly ignored. Cadmium poisoning caused intense pain to residents along the Jinzu River in Toyama prefecture. It came to be known as the "it hurts disease" (*itai-itai byo*). Yokkaichi (near Nagoya) and Kawasaki (near Yokohama) became infamous for smog and waterways where **aquatic life** disappeared. Fisheries in some areas became so polluted with cadmium and mercury that the fishermen went out of business entirely because the **fish and shellfish** were unfit for human consumption. Victims sought redress through protests and lawsuits, but typically the polluters denied responsibility and obstructed investigations. Both local governments and national administrators remained relatively passive.

But groups of pollution victims in the late 1960s began to build networks of support nationwide and organize boycotts and sit-ins. In 1967 the Diet at long last passed the comprehensive **Pollution Countermeasures Basic Law**, which became the base for numerous lawsuits against polluting enterprises brought by local resident activist groups. A series of landmark decisions between 1971 and 1973 gave victims the right to compensation and helped establish preventive measures against pollution. As a result, though the skies did not turn blue, the acrid smell decreased as did the yellowish gray smog.

安保

1960年に日米安全保障条約が改定されることになったとき、日本は正しい方向に向かっているという国民の総意とみなされたものにひずみが生じました。同年5月には反自民党勢力が、わずかばかり修正された安全保障条約の延長を遅らせるため、妨害行為や座り込みに訴えました。

学生たちは、この条約によって日米が反共産主義運動のもとに連携していると考え、リベラル派の知識人や労働組合の活動家と手を組んで条約に反対しました。彼らは、中立もしくは第三諸国との連帯を望んでいました。1959年初頭から、学生や学生に共鳴した人々は自分たちの目標を達成しようと、東京の街路、特に国会議事堂周辺で大規模デモを展開しました。

学生たちは条約締結を阻止できませんでした。当時の岸信介首相は強攻策を採り、警官隊を国会に入れて抵抗する反対議員を排除すると、出席していた自民党支持者のみによる強行採決を行いました。労働者は、首相が民主的手続きを完全に無視したことに憤慨してストに突入、数十万人もの学生が街頭デモに集まりました。東京では学生と機動隊が激突するなかで、当時22歳で東京大学4年の学生運動家、樺美智子さんが圧死し、危機はピークに達しました。彼女の死は国民の同情を集めただ

安保闘争。国会前で激しい衝突をする（1960年5月）

"Ampo"

When the U.S.–Japan Security Treaty came up for revision in 1960, cracks appeared in what had seemed to be a general consensus that Japan was headed in the right direction. Opponents of the LDP resorted to filibusters and **sit-ins** to delay the extension of a slightly revised security treaty in May 1960.

Students allied with liberal intellectuals and labor unionists to oppose the treaty because they believed it aligned Japan with the U.S. in an **anticommunist crusade**. For their part, they preferred either neutrality or alignment with the Third World. Beginning in 1959, students and their allies staged mass demonstrations in the streets of Tokyo, especially around the **Diet Building**, to promote their goals.

Student demonstrations failed to prevent passage of the treaty. Prime Minister Kishi Nobusuke resorted to heavy-handed methods to ram the bill through the National Diet, calling police into the Diet to drag opponents out and then calling a snap vote with only the LDP loyalists in attendance. Resenting the prime minister's complete disregard for democratic procedures, workers went on strike and hundreds of thousands of Japanese students swarmed through the streets in protest. The crisis reached a peak when a 22-year old University of Tokyo senior and student activist named

けでなく、条約改定に反対する世論をさらに
強化しました。多くの国民が不満を抱いてい
たにもかかわらず、安全保障条約は国会で批
准されました。

　　条約批准を阻止できなかったことに不満を
抱いた急進派の学生たちは、左翼組織の諸派
を結成しました。その後、彼らは地下活動を
続け、1960年代後半に世界各国の首都で学生
組織によるベトナム戦争反対運動が広まると、
再び台頭しました。

ベトナム戦争と反戦運動

　　東京オリンピックを通じて再び国際社会の
一員となったことを祝う間もなく、日本は大き
な国際的な試練に直面しました。米国のイン
ドシナ戦争（1963～1973年）の間、日本は経
済的、軍事的に重要なパートナーを務める立
場に置かれたのです。戦時中、日本は海外派兵
は行わなかったものの、軍事的な協力を行い、
軍需品の発注に対応し、いわゆる米兵の発着
拠点としての役割を果たしました。
　　羽田空港は、カリフォルニアからサイゴン
に飛ぶ兵員輸送機の給油基地として利用され
ました。立川飛行場の広大な土地は、補給司令
部、兵員・物資の輸送中継拠点となりました。

Kamba Michiko was crushed to death during a battle between students and riot police in Tokyo. Her death not only brought sympathy from the general public but further strengthened public opinion against the renewal of the security treaty. Despite broad public dissatisfaction the security treaty was passed by the Diet.

Frustrated by their failure to stop the **treaty passage**, radical students joined cells of factionalized leftists. They remained underground until the late 1960s when they emerged to protest the Vietnam War, as did student groups throughout the world's capitals.

Vietnam War and the Anti-war Movement

Hardly had Japan had time to celebrate its return to the international stage via the Tokyo Olympics than it faced a major international challenge. During America's war in Indochina (1965–1973), Japan was put in the position of serving as a major economic and military partner. Although Japan did not **send troops abroad** during the war, it furnished military collaboration, filled procurement orders and served as a kind of home base for **GIs**.

Haneda Airport served as a **refueling base** for soldiers flying from California to Saigon. A large airfield at Tachikawa served as a supply headquarters and transit point for personnel and material. Sagamihara served

ダナン北方39キロ地点に
上陸した米海兵隊
（1965年）

相模原基地は、戦車などの軍用車両の修理拠点でした。厚木の空軍基地は航空機用エンジンの整備工場の役割を果たしました。

沖縄はさらに大きな役割を果たしました。嘉手納基地に常備されたKC135空中給油隊は、グアムからインドシナの標的までの長距離を飛行するB52爆撃機に給油するために使われました。沖縄はベトナム戦争に加わる航空部隊の出撃拠点としての役割も果たし、1965年から1973年の間に100万件以上の飛行作戦が嘉手納基地から行われ、平均すると1日中3分ごとに爆撃機の離発着が行われていたことは、沖縄の重要性を示しています。

反戦・反基地運動家は東京に集中しており、彼らは日本の「間接的」軍事的関与を指摘しました。例えば、安全保障条約では「日本から行われる軍事戦闘作戦」は日本政府の事前の合意が必要と定められています。実際には、陸上部隊または爆撃機が日本から出発した後に指令を出した場合、**事前協議**は必ずしも必要ではなかったのです。条約を寛大に解釈すれば、**日本の領空**を飛び立った後に発令されれば、東京に配備された飛行機が日本政府との事前協議なくベトナムを爆撃することも可能でした。

第2の焦点は、日本が国内への核兵器持ち込みを拒否していたことです。核搭載が可能な米国の軍用機、潜水艦、艦船も、実際に核兵器を搭載していなければ、事前協議なく日

as a repair point for damaged tanks and other military vehicles. An air base at Atsugi served as a complete repair shop for jet engines.

Okinawa played an even larger role. A squadron of KC-135 tanker planes based at Kadena were used to refuel B-52 bombers during their long flights from Guam to targets in Indochina. Okinawa also served as the jumping-off point for American combat troops entering the Vietnam War, and illustrating Okinawa's importance was the fact that during the period 1965–1973 more than a million flight operations took place from Kadena—averaging a landing or takeoff every three minutes around the clock.

The **anti-war and anti-base activists** were concentrated in Tokyo, and they called attention to Japan's "indirect" involvement in the war. For example, the security treaty required that any "military combat operations to be undertaken from Japan" had to be discussed with the Japanese government in advance. In actual fact, no **prior consultation** was essential, *if* the actual orders for combat were issued after the troops or bombers had left Japan. With this **lenient** interpretation of the treaty, an airplane based in Tokyo could bomb Vietnam without advance consultation with the Japanese government, if the orders were issued after leaving **Japanese air space**.

A second issue was Japan's stated refusal to allow nuclear weapons into the country. Any U.S. plane, submarine or naval vessel capable of carrying nuclear weapons would be allowed to enter Japan without prior

本入国が許可されました。日本政府は国民に、「米国政府が事前協議を提起してこない以上、核の持ち込みはない」と繰り返し説明しました。しかし、米国の軍艦が日本の港や空港を訪れる前に、わざわざ核兵器を下ろしてはいないことは実際には明らかでした。

第3に運動家たちは、日本企業が米国の軍用機器を供給し、直接的な調達と、物資・サービス提供の両面から利益を得ているという点を指摘しました。これらのなかには、薬品、消費材、車両部品、機械、電気ケーブルの輸出も含まれていました。日本経済が直接・間接調達から得た収益については、一般的な見解として、米軍とその関連産業への輸出が全輸出の7%を占めていました。米国がベトナムに軍事介入している間、日本は積極的な同盟国ではなかったかもしれませんが、紛争の恩恵については主要国だったのかもしれません。

大学の騒乱

1968、69年は日本の高等教育に深い傷を残しました。学生デモはそれまでの数十年間、政治機構を標的としてきましたが、この2年間、標的は大学そのものでした。問題となったのは、旧態依然とした大学制度、教育問題に対す

consultation, as long as it did not actually have such nuclear weapons on board. The Japanese government repeatedly told the people that since there had been no prior consultations, the vessels and planes that did enter must be free of such weapons. It became fairly clear, however, that U.S. vessels were not going to the trouble to offload such weapons before visiting Japanese ports and airports.

Third, Protestors pointed out that Japanese companies were supplying the U.S. war machine and profiting from both direct procurements and the provision of goods and services. Among these items were exports of chemicals, consumer goods, vehicle parts, machinery and electrical cable. Estimates of how much the Japanese economy profited from the direct and indirect procurements vary, but a consensus is that as much as 7% of Japan's exports went to the U.S. military and related industries. Japan may have been a reluctant ally during the American involvement in Vietnam, but Japan may have been the chief beneficiary of the conflict.

University Upheavals

The years 1968 and 1969 were **traumatic** in Japanese higher education. Student demonstrations had for decades targeted political organizations, but during these two years in particular the target became the universities themselves. Among the issues were the antiquated

る国の怠慢、画一的な「マスプロ」教育、不十分な設備でした。大きな問題はいわゆる「**受験地獄**」と、それに伴うすべてのものでした。極めて難しい入学試験に合格することは、学校への入学だけでなく、生涯の社会的地位や経済的成功を決定づけるものでした。大学をとりまく諸問題は、ベトナム戦争への反対や沖縄返還要求、安全保障条約反対とも絡み合っていきました。

　多くのデモは平和的なものでしたが、多くの大学が授業を停止し、学生は締め出されることを余儀なくされました。最も鮮烈な印象を残した紛争は、学生による東京大学の中心的建物の占拠でした。

　東大の紛争は1968年6月、医学部のインターン登録制度が発端となり、すぐに全学へと広がり、一般学生のストライキを起こしました。学生たちは大学当局の改正に譲歩しましたが、全共闘（全学共闘会議）の**過激派学生**たちは、占拠していた大学の主要建物である安田講堂から撤退することを拒否しました。

　1969年1月18日と19日、それまで過激派と直接交渉を続けることで自治を保ってきた大学当局は、政府に対し、バリケード封鎖する過激派を撤去させるよう要請しました。機動隊8000人が建物に入り、600人以上の学生が排除、逮捕されました。この2日間の激しい攻防戦を、何百万

東大紛争。赤門横で集会中の一般学生たちと小競り合いする反日共系学生たち（1968年）

nature of the university system, national neglect of educational problems, "mass production" education and inadequate school facilities. A major issue was the so-called "**examination hell**" and all that it implied. Success on excessively difficult exams determined not only entrance to the school but social and economic status for life. Mixed into the university-centered issues were protests against the Vietnam War, calls for the reversion of Okinawa and protests against the Security Treaty.

Many demonstrations were peaceful, but many universities were forced to suspend classes and lock out students. The major image of the struggle was the student seizure of a central building at the University of Tokyo.

The troubles at Todai began in June 1968 over the internship admissions process at the medical school, but controversy soon spread throughout the university and resulted in a general student strike. Students accepted concessions for reform from university authorities, but **radical students** of Zenkyoto (*Zengaku Kyoto Kaigi*), the All Student Joint Struggle Council, refused to leave Yasuda Hall, the main university building which they had occupied.

On January 18 and 19, 1969, the university authorities, who until then had attempted to maintain its autonomy by dealing directly with the radicals, called on the government to remove the barricaded radicals. A task force of 8,000 police moved in to remove and arrest more than 600 students. The two-day violent assault was watched by millions on television. Those convicted in the court cases that followed later found it difficult to

もの人々がテレビ中継で見守りました。裁判で有罪となった者はその後、大企業への就職が難しくなりました。

東大の紛争は次第に沈静化しましたが、その年の春の入学試験は中止されました。入学試験の廃止を紛争の目標の一つとしていた過激派学生たちは、これを勝利とし、ほかの大学の入試を阻む運動にも乗り出しました。

1970年以降、大学は平穏になりましたが、過激派はその後も闘争を続け、しばしば暴力的行為を行い、その矛先を他の党派や企業に向けました。

東京オリンピック

1964年10月10日に開会された東京オリンピックは、戦争の敗北と戦後の絶望的な状況から復興し、世界の舞台に戻った日本を祝福するものとして、大いに期待され、入念に準備されました。アジアで初めて開催されたこのオリンピックは、めざましい経済復興の成果を日本人と世界の人々に披露する場となりました。

昭和天皇は**大会名誉総裁**として表舞台に立ち、かつての帝国建設者ではなく、いまや復興を遂げた平和国家の立派な先導者であることを世界に示しました。

find employment with major corporations.

The troubles at Todai gradually came to an end, but the spring entrance exams that year had to be cancelled. Since radical students had taken the abolition of entrance exams as one of their goals, they took this as a victory and launched campaigns to block the entrance exams at other universities as well.

After 1970 the universities quieted, but radicals continued their struggle, often committing violence and often turning violent against other factions and against businesses.

The Tokyo Olympic Games

The Tokyo Olympic Games, opened on October 10, 1964, were much anticipated and carefully designed to celebrate Japan's recovery from defeat in wartime and desperate conditions after the war and its return to the

東京オリンピック。金メダルに輝いた女子バレーボールチーム。壇上は河西
（1964年）

1964年10月1日に開通した東海道新幹線「こだま」は東京—大阪間を高速で結びました。開業当初の営業最高速度は200km/h、現在は約1.5倍の300km/hで運行しています。

高い安全性とスピードを兼ね備えた技術は台湾、英国、中国など海外にも輸出されるなど世界でも注目を集めています。

新幹線こだま号（1964年）

オリンピック開会式の10日前には東京—大阪間に新幹線が開通し、東西二大都市がそれまでは想像もつかなかった3時間10分という短時間で結ばれました。東京—名古屋間には近代的で新しい高速道路が開通しました。東京では、地下鉄が開通・延長され、各開催地に通じるようになりました。

「ニクソン・ショック」

日本経済は、10%の年間成長率を維持するだろうという予測のもと、順調に1970年代を迎えたように見えましたが、幾つかの出来事で楽観的観測には根拠がないことが分かりました。

1971年にリチャード・ニクソン米大統領が、米国が金本位制を廃止し、**ドル—円の固定相場制**の解消を示唆する発表を行ったことで、最初の衝撃が走りました。米国政府は日本

world stage. The first games to be held in Asia, they were an occasion to show off the fruits of an amazing economic recovery, both to themselves and to the world at large.

The emperor was given a highly visible role as **official Patron of the Games** and the world was shown that the former empire-builder was now a dignified leader of a rehabilitated and peace-loving Japan.

Ten days before the Olympic Opening Ceremony, the Shinkansen "Bullet Trains" went into operation between Tokyo and Osaka, tying those cities in the unheard-of time of three hours and ten minutes. A modern new expressway linked Tokyo with Nagoya. Tokyo opened new and extended subway lines to serve the various venues.

"Nixon Shocks"

The Japanese economy seemed to race along into the 1970s, with expectations of a continued annual growth of 10%, but several events proved that optimism to be unfounded.

The first shock was the President Richard Nixon's announcement in 1971 that the U.S. was abandoning the **gold standard**, signaling a dissolution of the **fixed dollar–yen exchange rate**. In order to assist Japan in its

が経済復興し、占領終了後に国を再建するの
を支援するため、1ドル＝360円という意図的
に低く見積もった為替レートを維持してきま
した。この不自然な為替レートは、1971年ま
で日本の輸出に大きな恩恵をもたらしました。
同時に米国は、1950年代から1960年代にか
けて、日本製品がほとんど規制されずに米国
消費市場に入り、また日本が自動車などの輸
入品に規制を設けることを許容してきました。

　1971年までに、日本は完全に復活したかの
ように見えました。人為的な保護は撤廃され、
円のドルに対する変動相場制が始まりました。
米国が「同盟国」の日本と協議せずに単独で決
定を下したことも、ニクソン声明の「ショック」
でした。1972年1月までには、1ドル＝312円
に円は上昇し、以後10年間でさらに強くなりま
した（1980年代初めに1ドル＝237円、1990年
には144円、2000年には105円になりました）。

　1971年7月、米国政府が長く非友好的態度
をとってきた中国を訪問するとニクソンが電
撃発表したことで、衝撃はさらに続きました。
このときもまた、日本との事前協議も事前の通
告さえもないまま、劇的な発表がなされたので
す。米国が日本をまったく信頼していない、つ
まり同等のパートナーとして見ていないこと
は、日本の批評家にとって明らかでした。

　これらの批評家たちを苛立たせたのは、国
内に相当な反対があったにもかかわらず、日
本政府が中国の共産党政府を「牽制」する米国
の政策に忠実に従ってきたことでした。米国

economic recovery and the reconstruction of the nation after the Occupation, the U.S. maintained a deliberately undervalued exchange rate of ¥360 to $1. This unnatural rate benefited Japanese exports enormously until 1971. At the same time, the U.S. through the 1950s and 1960s allowed Japanese manufacturers nearly open access to the American consumer market, while allowing Japan to restrict imports such as automobiles.

By 1971, Japan was seen as having completed its comeback. The artificial protections were eliminated, beginning with the flotation of the yen against the dollar. Part of the "shock" of Nixon's announcement was that the U.S. had acted unilaterally, without consulting its "ally." By January 1972, the yen had risen to ¥312 to the dollar and strengthened further over the decade. (At the beginning of 1980 that rate had slid to ¥237, by 1990 to ¥144, and by 2000 to ¥105.)

The shockwaves continued with Nixon's shock announcement in July 1971 of his plan to travel to the People's Republic of China, the nation the U.S. had long vilified. Once again, the dramatic announcement had been made without prior consultation with or even prior notice to the Japanese government. It appeared obvious to critics in Japan that America either did not fully trust Japan or did not regard it as an equal partner.

What irritated these critics was that despite considerable domestic opposition, the Japanese government had loyally followed America's lead in "containing" the Communist government of China. When the American

が唐突に方針を覆したことで、日本の指導者たちはいわゆる「同盟国」に顔をつぶされたのです。政権を握って2カ月足らずだった田中角栄首相は、直ちに国際政治の急変に対応し、米国に従って中国を承認することを決断しました。この決断は国内での田中の人気を高めました。1972年9月、田中は北京を訪問して**日中共同声明**に調印しました。これにより、外交使節を交換し、中華人民共和国が中国の唯一の合法政府であり、台湾に対する主権を有するとみなし、日中両国間の国交を回復しました。その後、1978年に両国は**日中平和友好条約**を締結し、両国間の国交は完全に正常化しました。

これらの「衝撃」が日本に与えたより複雑な影響は、日本が明らかに一層豊かになっていく一方、その繁栄は、政治的にも経済的にも、国際社会の変化に大きく影響を受けるものであったことが認識されたことでした。

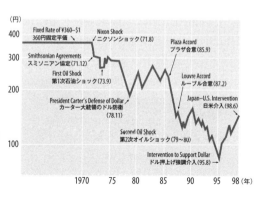

円―ドルレートの変遷
Value of Yen in
Relation to Dollar

*IMFデータより

position suddenly reversed, Japanese leaders were left embarrassed by their so-called "ally." In quick response to the changing international political climate, Prime Minister Tanaka Kakuei, who had assumed power a scant two months earlier, decisively followed suit by recognizing the People's Republic of China, a decision that made him highly popular at home. Traveling to Beijing in September 1972, Tanaka signed a **joint communiqué** providing for the exchange of diplomats and recognition of the People's Republic of China as the sole government of China, with sovereignty over Taiwan. Later, in 1978, the two nations signed the **China–Japan Peace and Friendship Treaty**, completely normalizing relations between the two nations.

A more subtle impact of these "shocks" was the realization that although Japan was clearly growing more affluent, that prosperity was highly vulnerable to changes in the international scene, both political and economic.

オイルショック

1973年、石油輸出国機構（OPEC）は突然、原油価格を70%近く引き上げました。日本は、産業用原油を完全に輸入に依存し、かつ禁輸対象国に含まれることを予想していなかったため、この値上げは「オイルショック」として知られるようになりました。「オイルショック」は、日本が相互に依存する世界のなかの、資源に乏しい経済国であるという現実を浮き彫りにしました。古い世代は戦中・戦後の物不足を思い起こしました。消費者は日用品を買いだめするようになり、新聞は主婦が洗剤やトイレットペーパーといった日常生活の必需品を買い占める写真を掲載しました。

「オイルショック」は経済不況をもたらしましたが、それは一時的なものでした。逆に、「オイルショック」によって、日本の自動車メーカーは米国で自動車を販売する好機を見出し、燃費の良い日本車はデトロイト産のガソリンを喰う自動車に慣れていた米国人にとってはより魅力的でした。今や「メイド・イン・ジャパン」

オイルショック。店員の制止も聞かずトイレットペーパーなど石油製品の売り場に殺到するお客さん。
東京・青山のスーパーで（1973年11月）

は信頼、高品質、比較的に低い価格を意味し、1980年までに日本は世界のどの国よりも多くの車を売るようになりました。1983年にはトヨタと日産が世界の自動車メーカーでそれぞれ2位、3位となり、1980年代の終わりには日本の自動車メーカーが米国市

The Oil Shock

In 1973 the Organization of Petroleum Exporting Countries suddenly increased the price of **crude oil** nearly 70%. To Japan, completely dependent on imported petroleum for its industries and not expecting to be included in the OPEC oil embargo, this rise became known as the "oil shock." The "oil shock" highlighted the fact that Japan remained a resource-poor economy in an **interdependent** world. It reminded an older generation of the scarcity of goods in wartime and the postwar period. Consumers began to **hoard** goods and newspapers carried photographs of housewives buying up entire stocks of essential items of everyday life such as laundry detergent and toilet paper.

The result of the "oil shock" was a contraction of the economy, but only a brief one. To the contrary, the "oil shock" provided an opportunity for Japanese automobile manufacturers to sell cars in the U.S. Smaller, **more fuel-efficient** Japanese cars were suddenly more appealing to Americans than the gas-guzzlers that Detroit produced. "Made in Japan" now signified reliability, high quality and relatively low prices, so by 1980 Japan was selling more automobiles than any other nation in the world. By 1983 Toyota and Nissan ranked number two and three among automakers in the world, and by the end of the decade, Japanese automakers held almost 25% of the U.S. market.

場のほぼ25%を占めるまでになりました。

　電機メーカーでは、松下幸之助がフィリップス社と技術提携を行い、テレビ、オーディオ製品、冷蔵庫、洗濯機などの家電の生産に乗り出しました。松下電器産業は、1955年から1960年の間に売上げを7倍に増やしました。パナソニックとナショナルのブランド名で市場に出された電気製品も米国市場を席巻し、米国の消費者がこの会社──そして競合企業のソニー──は米国のメーカーだと思うほどでした。

　「オイルショック」により経済は停滞し、1974年の成長率は実質ゼロでしたが、1974年以降、15年間にわたって日本のGNPは毎年平均4%成長しました。この成長率は「高度成長」の時代に比べると低いものでしたが、それでも同時期の米国、西ドイツ、英国の成長率の倍でした。日本人が「わずか」3〜6%の年間成長率に落胆していた一方で、諸外国はその「抜きん出た経済力」を羨望していたのです。

三島由紀夫事件・あさま山荘事件

　1970年11月、作家の三島由紀夫は、自ら結成した超国粋主義団体「楯の会」を率いて東京・市ヶ谷の**陸上自衛隊**の駐屯地に乗り込み、戦前の政治的秩序を復活させようとしました。本館のバルコニーから自衛隊員に演説する彼を迎え

Among the electronic manufacturers, Matsushita Konosuke linked up with Philip's technology to introduce home electrical appliances like televisions, audio equipment, refrigerators and washing machines. Matsushita Electric Industrial Company saw sales increase seven times over between 1955 and 1960. Marketed under the brand names Panasonic and National, electronic goods also flooded the American market, to such a degree that American consumers thought the company—and its rival Sony—were American manufacturers.

While the "oil shock" stunned the economy, which did not grow at all in 1974, in the fifteen-year period that followed 1974, the GNP grew at an average rate of 4% each year. While this was low compared to the period of "high growth," it was still double the rate of growth in the U.S., West Germany and England during that period. While the Japanese may have felt disappointment at a "mere" 3–6% per year, the rest of the world was envious of this "superior economic performance."

Shocks of a Different Sort

In November 1970, the novelist Mishima Yukio led his private ultranationalist group "Tate no Kai" to the **Ground Self-Defense Force** headquarters in Ichigaya, Tokyo and attempted to provoke a restoration of the prewar political order. Addressing the troops from the

陸上自衛隊市ヶ谷駐屯地
で演説をぶつ三島由紀夫
（1970年11月）

たのは、まったくの**無関心**でした。自衛隊員を
奮起させることに失敗した彼は切腹の儀式を行
いました。現代にこのような伝統的な行為が行
われたことに、日本人は衝撃を受けましたが、
三島の芝居がかった戦前回帰の呼びかけには
共感しませんでした。海外の人々も驚き、日本
に軍国主義が復活するのではないかと懸念しま
した。

　1972年には左翼が注目を浴びました。日本
の米軍基地、日米安全保障条約、沖縄、中国、
そして1973年の米国のベトナム撤退といった
最も**刺激的な**平和問題について、対処できな
くなっていた暴力的な左翼は、その戦術と怒
りをほかのセクトに向けました。

　1972年の過激派による暴力事件の一つに、
後に**あさま山荘事件**として知られる、軽井沢に
ある保養所の管理人の妻を人質に取り、警察隊

🔖 よど号ハイジャック事件

　1970年3月、日本赤軍のメンバー9人は、日本航空の東京発福岡行き旅
客機「よど号」をハイジャックし、世界を震撼させる事件を引き起こしま
した。これらメンバーのほとんどが様々な容疑で指名手配されており、彼
らは飛行機を乗っ取って国外に逃亡する決意を固めているようでした。ハ
イジャックによって自分たちの名を世に知らしめることも目的でした。

　彼らはハイジャックすると、福岡空港で給油をさせ、人質の一部を解放
するとともに、北朝鮮に向かうよう要求しました。旅客機は離陸し、秘密
裏に韓国の空港に誘導されました。しかし赤軍のメンバーたちは駐機して
いる米軍機を目にし、そこが北朝鮮ではないことに気づいたのです。最終
的に彼らは北朝鮮に降り立つことを許されました。

　日本政府は、北朝鮮に犯人の引き渡しを要求しましたが、北朝鮮政府は

balcony of the main building, he was met with **indifference**. Failing to stir the troops, he committed ritual *seppuku*, slicing his belly open with a sword. The Japanese public was shocked that this traditional act was committed in modern times, but they were nevertheless unsympathetic to Mishima's theatrical call to restoration. The public abroad was also alarmed, worried about the possible revival of militarism in Japan.

The Left had its own moments in the spotlight during 1972. Having lost control of the most **evocative** peace issues—U.S. bases in Japan, the U.S.–Japan Security Treaty, Okinawa and China, and in 1973 the Vietnam War after America withdrew from Vietnam—the violent leftists turned their tactics and anger toward other factions.

Among the violent incidents committed by radicals in 1972 was the kidnapping of the wife of a hotel manager of a Karuizawa, in what became known as the

日本警察の肩代わりを拒否すると回答してきました。その結果、彼らハイジャック犯グループは北朝鮮に留まりました。

彼らが金日成の思想を受け入れ、北朝鮮政府に代わって日本にその思想を広める活動を行っていることが最近になって明らかになりました。

2001年5月には、ハイジャック犯の娘3人が来日したと報じられ、このハイジャック事件が再び注目されました。北朝鮮で生まれ育ったとしても、日本人の子どもである彼女たちは当然ながら日本の国籍を持っていたのです。

国際手配中のハイジャック犯人

バンチボールで屋根の一部
が崩れ落ちたあさま山荘
（1972年2月28日）

と銃撃戦となった事件がありました。

　その前年、日本と海外の人々を深く震撼させ
たのは、日本赤軍がテルアビブのロッド空港を
襲撃した事件でした。日本人過激派3人がパレ
スチナ解放運動に加わり、テルアビブに渡って、
荷物カウンター周辺にいた旅行者に向けて**無差
別**に発砲し、26人を殺害しました。

元日本兵の帰国

　第2次世界大戦の終結から27年、元大日本
帝国陸軍兵がグアム島のジャングルから救出
されました。かつて洋服の仕立屋だった横井
庄一さん（当時56歳）は、靴、衣類、ロープの
ほか、80点もの生活必需品を自分で作り、ほ
ぼ30年間完全に孤立した環境で生き延びまし
た。日本の人々は、彼の生命力と任務への一意
専心に驚嘆しました。

　日本に帰国した直後、彼は「恥ずかしなが
ら、生きて帰ってまいりました」と宣言して
人々を驚かせました。「恥ずかしながら」は、
戦争を生き延び、任務遂行に命を捧げなかっ
た軍人がかつてよく使った言葉で、日本の
人々には長く忘れられていました。それは、東
条英機首相の下で、すべての兵士は「生きて虜
囚の辱を受けず」と促す有名な**戦陣訓**を陸軍

Asama Lodge Incident, resulting in an exchange of gunfire with police.

Deeply disturbing to people abroad and at home was the Japanese Red Army attack on Lod Airport in Tel Aviv that year before. Three Japanese radicals joined the Palestine liberation movement, traveled to Tel Aviv where they opened fire **indiscriminately** on travelers in the baggage area, killing 26 people.

Return of Yokoi Shoichi (1972) and Onoda Hiroo (1974)

Twenty-eight years after the end of World War II, a former Japanese Imperial Army soldier was rescued from a jungle cave on Guam. A former tailor, Yokoi Shoichi, aged 56, had made his own shoes, his own clothing, rope and 80 other essential items for daily life and survived in complete isolation for almost three decades. The Japanese public was astounded at both his ability to survive and his **single-minded devotion** to duty.

Upon his return to Japan, he surprised the public by declaring, "I am ashamed to say that I returned home having prolonged my life." The phrase "I am ashamed," once common among military men who survived the war and had not given their lives in fulfilling their duty, had been long forgotten by the Japanese public. It referred to the fact that under Prime Minister Tojo, the army had issued a famous **field code** in which

フィリピンのルバング島で
孤独な戦いを続け、29年
ぶりの敗戦を迎えた小野田
寛郎元陸軍少尉（1974年）

が発令していたことによるものでした。しか
し横井さんは、自分がいなかった間に起きて
いたことをすぐ理解し、後に「私は人生の半分
を無駄にした」とも語りました。

　それから2年後の1974年3月には、もう一
人の元日本兵、小野田寛郎さんがフィリピン
のジャングルから姿を現しました。小野田さ
んと数人の**敗残兵**は、日本が戦争に敗れたこ
とを知っていましたが、小野田さんは任務解
除命令を受けていないという理由から戦闘を
続けました。任務を遂行するために、彼はわず
かな所持品を背負ってジャングルを転々とし、
野生的な生活を送り、ときには地元の村を**襲
撃する**こともありました。小野田さんは、一度
そのような敗残兵を探していた日本人と接触
したこともありましたが、直属の上官からの
直接の降伏命令がないまま刀も銃も置くこと
は拒否しました。その上官は生還しており、彼
は小野田さんに直接に任務解除命令を下すた
めにフィリピンに飛びました。

　ほぼ30年間、小野田さんは「1人だけの日
本軍」を自任し、帝国陸軍の精神を体現しまし
た。彼の態度は1974年の日本の現実からはる
かにかけ離れていたため、彼の突然の帰還は、
天皇と日本社会の関係について白熱した議論
のきっかけとなりました。

　三島の自殺と同様、2人の陸軍兵が過去の
奥底から突然現れたことは、多くの日本人を
驚かせ、すでに慣れ親しんだ近代的、物質的な

all fighting men were encouraged to "not live to incur the shame of becoming a prisoner." However, it was not long before Yokoi realized what had happened during his absence and he would later comment, "I wasted half of my life."

Two years later, in March 1974, another former soldier, Onoda Hiroo, walked out of the jungles of the Philippines. He and several other **stragglers** had known that Japan had lost the war, but Onoda continued to fight because he had not received orders relieving them of duty. In order to perform his duties, he had moved from place to place in the jungle with their meager possessions on his back, living off the land and occasionally **raiding** local villages. Onoda, once contacted by Japanese hunting for such stragglers, refused to lay down his sword or rifle without a direct order to surrender from his immediate superior officer. The officer in question had survived the war, and he flew to the Philippines in order to directly relieve Onoda of his duties.

For almost three decades, Onoda had considered himself a "one-man Japanese army," embodying the spirit of the imperial army. Because his attitude was so far removed from the reality of Japan in 1974, his sudden reappearance stimulated heated discussion about how the emperor and Japanese society were related.

Along with Mishima's suicide, the sudden appearance of two imperial army soldiers from the depths of the past stunned many Japanese and called into

戦後文化への疑問を呼びました。しかし一般
庶民の圧倒的多数にとっては、これら「過去の
亡霊」は、終戦後日本がいかに「進歩」したか
を**明らかにした**だけでした。

沖縄返還

　1950年代、1960年代を通じて、米国に対す
る日本の「**従属的独立**」が比較的うまく機能し
ていると感じていた日本人もいました。経済
界の指導層は、米国の**軍事的庇護**の下にある
ことがいかに高度成長と貿易の成功に貢献し
ているかを理解していました。反軍国主義者
たちは、米国の存在が日本の自らの軍隊を持
つことの必要性を緩和し、軍事的な非常事態
に日本が米国に依存できるからこそ憲法第9
条が的確に機能していると感じていました。

　しかし、日本に軍事的脅威が直接及んだ場
合、米軍が実際にそれを阻止するのか、疑いを
抱く人々もいました。逆に、米軍の存在は日本
を望まない戦争に引き込むのではないか、も
しくは最悪の場合、核戦争が起きた場合に日
本を危険にさらすのではないか、と懸念しま
した。そのような懸念を裏付ける証拠も出て
きました。例えば、米国の**U2偵察機**が旧ソ連
で撃墜されたU2機事件です。米軍のU2機が
3機、日本の基地に駐留していたことがその後

question the modern, materialistic postwar culture that they had grown accustomed to. But for the vast majority of the populace, these "ghosts from the past" only served to **illustrate** how much "progress" had been made since the end of the war.

The Reversion of Okinawa

Throughout the 1950s and 1960s, some Japanese felt that Japan's **"subordinate independence"** vis-à-vis the U.S. worked relatively well. Business leaders saw how being under America's **military umbrella** contributed to high-speed growth and prosperous trade. Anti-militarists felt that the American presence alleviated the need for Japan to have its own military and that Article 9 worked precisely because Japan could fall back on the U.S. in a military emergency.

But there were others who doubted whether U.S. forces would actually deter direct military threats to Japan. To the contrary, they worried that the presence of American troops might draw Japan into an unwanted conflict, or, in a worse-case scenario, place Japan in danger during a nuclear conflict. Evidence supporting such worries appeared, for example, in the U-2 Incident, in which a U-2 **spy plane** was shot down in the Soviet Union. It was later disclosed that three other American U-2s were stationed in Japan. The American authorities

沖縄返還対策のために使われている米陸軍の教育用テキスト（1972年5月）

明らかにされました。米国政府は、日本の基地から飛行したU2機は**気象観測**をしていただけだと言明し、岸首相も、自身が知る限り、日本に駐留するU2機が他国の領空を侵犯したことはないと述べました。しかし日本人の大半はどちらの主張にも納得できませんでした。旧ソ連は、U2機が自国の領空を侵犯したのだから、日本の基地を報復攻撃する可能性もあると警告しました。

小笠原諸島と沖縄は、日米安全保障条約により米国の施政権下におかれました。米国政府は、沖縄を植民地のように扱い、島中に陸海空軍それぞれの基地を設けました。小笠原諸島は1968年、沖縄は1972年にそれぞれ日本に返還され、日本人の不安はいくらか解消されました。

しかし、米軍基地には条約の合意が適用されたままで、基地外で米兵が関与するトラブルや基地の騒音といった問題も後を絶たず、議論を呼んでいます。1996年時点では、米軍基地が沖縄県全土の10.4%を占め、米軍が占

🔖 U2偵察機

U2偵察機は、1955年に米空軍とCIAに採用された高高度偵察機です。U2は偵察用の特殊なカメラでソ連など冷戦対立国の弾道ミサイルなどの軍事配備を撮影しました。また、米ソの冷戦のターニングポイントに数回登場しました。U2は撃墜されないように高高度を飛行する偵察機ですが、ソ連は有効な地対空ミサイルを開発し、1960年には領空侵犯を行っていたCIA所属のU2を撃墜しました。1962年には、米国と対立していたキュー

stated that the U-2s operating from Japanese bases had been engaged in **weather observation** only, and Prime Minister Kishi stated that, as far as he knew, U-2s based in Japan had never invaded the air space of other countries. But most Japanese remained unconvinced by such assurances. The Soviet Union warned of possible retaliation against Japanese bases because U-2 planes had invaded Soviet air space.

The security treaty between America and Japan had left the Ogasawara Islands and Okinawa in the hands of the Americans. The U.S. government ran Okinawa like a colonial territory, building bases for each of the armed forces all over the island. A portion of the Japanese concern was removed when the Ogasawara Islands were returned to Japanese sovereignty in 1968 and Okinawa was returned in 1972.

The U.S. bases, however, remained under the treaty agreement and problems involving U.S. personnel off base and noise from the bases continue to raise controversy. In 1996 the American bases occupied some 10.4% of Okinawa prefecture's total acreage and 75%

バで、ソ連が建設中のミサイル基地や弾道ミサイルがU2によって発見されました。その情報により、米国国防総省やCIAは攻撃を主張しましたが、当時のケネディ大統領は海上封鎖でソ連船の入港を拒否するにとどめました。その後、極度に緊迫した2週間余りの期間を経て、ソ連はフルシチョフがキューバからのミサイル撤退を表明し、交渉の結果米ソ両国の戦争は回避されました。U2はまさに冷戦という時代の鍵を握る「戦闘機」だったのです。

める日本の土地の75%が沖縄に集中していま
した。

貿易摩擦

　終戦直後の時期には、日本の対米貿易は輸
入が輸出を上回っていました。しかし1965年
にはこれが逆転し、それ以降、輸出は毎年増大
しました。1970年代までには、品質と付加価
値が向上した日本製品が米国市場に溢れまし
た。日本人との新たな激しい競争に直面した
米国企業や労働組合は、**不公正な取引**と考え
られるものについて不満を提起するようにな
りました。彼らは、日本のメーカーが保護され
た国内市場で高価格を設定しつつ、米国市場
ではシェア獲得のためにかなり低い価格で製
品を「ダンピング」している、と非難しました。
日本企業は米国企業を倒産させ、米国人労働
者を失業に追い込んでいるというのです。日本
の輸出業者が単に頭が切れるのか、あるいは
実際に非倫理的なのかは、見方の問題でした。
　「**貿易摩擦**」は、繊維（1972年）、鉄鋼（1969
年、1978年）、カラーテレビ（1977年）、自動
車（1981年）をめぐる日米間の政治的交渉に
発展しました。日本が**輸入規制**していたオレ
ンジ・牛肉（1988年）とコメ（1993年）が協議
され、前者は日本市場の全面開放、後者は部分
開放という結果になりました。日本車の輸出

of the land in Japan occupied by the American military was in that one prefecture.

Trade Friction

During the immediate postwar era, Japan imported more from the U.S. than it exported to the U.S. But in 1965 that trend reversed and every year thereafter saw an increase in exports. By the 1970s, Japan was flooding the American market with manufactured products of increasing quality and value. Faced with this new tough competition from the Japanese, American companies and labor unions began to complain about what they saw as **unfair trade**. They accused Japanese manufacturers, with considerable justification, of charging high prices in the protected Japanese market, while "dumping" products at far lower prices in order to win a share of the American market. They charged that Japanese companies were driving American companies out of business and pushing American workers out of jobs. Whether Japanese exporters were simply smart or actually unethical depended on which viewpoint one took.

The "**trade conflict**" led to political negotiations between Japan and the U.S. over textiles (1972), steel (1969 and 1978), color televisions (1977) and automobiles (1981). Conflict over Japanese **restrictions of imports** of oranges and beef (1988) and rice (1993) led to opening of Japan's market to the former and partial

交渉は、貿易摩擦が解決にいたるまでの一般的なパターンを示しています。

手頃な価格と高い信頼性で日本車の人気が高まると、米国との深刻な貿易問題が生じました。米国の自動車メーカーは日本企業との競争を懸念して、その経済問題を政治的に解決しようとしました。日本企業を不当に優遇しているとして、米国の自動車メーカーは、日本車の対米輸出の「**自主規制**」実施を交渉するよう米国政府に働きかけました。

米国の批判を真っ向から受けたかつての日本企業とは異なり、日本の自動車メーカーは自らの微妙な立場を踏まえ、すでに米国市場への適応に成功していたところに新たな戦略を加えました。彼らは米国で自社工場を建設し始め、そこで米国人労働者を雇用して自動車を生産し、現地市場で販売することで、自主規制や関税などの貿易障壁の影響を受けずに済んだのです。皮肉なことに、1980年代初頭に保護主義的な傾向の高まっていた米国の貿易環境は、日本の対米投資レベルをさらに

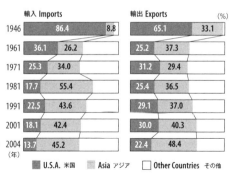

日本の地域別輸出入割合
Japanese Import and
Export Rates by Regions

*財務省・日本銀行データより

■ U.S.A. 米国　■ Asia アジア　□ Other Countries その他

opening to the latter. The example of negotiations over automobile exports illustrates the general pattern for reaching a solution to the conflicts.

The popularity of Japanese automobiles because of their reasonable cost and increasing reliability eventually provoked serious trade problems with the U.S. Concerned about competition from Japanese companies, American car manufacturers looked for political solutions to their economic problems. Claiming unfair advantages were being allowed to the Japanese, the American auto companies persuaded the American government to negotiate "**voluntary restraints**" on the export of Japanese cars to the U.S.

Unlike earlier Japanese manufacturers who had faced American criticism, Japanese auto makers, realizing the delicacy of their position, added a new strategy to their successful adaptations. They began to build their own factories in the U.S. where they could produce cars made by American workers and sell them in the market country where they would not be subject to voluntary restraints, tariffs or other trade barriers. Ironically, the more protectionist trade environment that developed in the U.S. during the early 1980s actually promoted higher levels of Japanese investment in the U.S. and strengthened the interdependence of the two economies **in unexpected ways**. Electrical manufacturers like Hitachi and Toshiba followed a similar **trajectory**.

引き上げ、**予期せぬ方法**で日米経済の相互依存を強化させました。日立や東芝などの電機メーカーも同様の**軌跡**を辿りました。

ロッキード事件と田中角栄

1960年代と1970年代には、「**金権政治**」は特に難しい問題となりました。国会議員選挙で当選するには膨大な費用がかかり、たとえ当選しても、議員に期待を寄せる**地元選挙区**に配慮するためには、さらに多額の金が必要でした。政治家は、地元の慈善事業に寄付をしたり、地元産業を支援したり、結婚式や祭事に贈答品を送るなどして、地元の支持を得ました。こうした出費を賄うには莫大な**現金収入**を必要とし、しばしば裕福な経営者や企業からの金が充てられました。もちろん、このような「献金」は関連法案での便宜供与を金で買うものだと見なされていました。

おそらく田中角栄首相にまつわるスキャンダルほど、世間の注目を集めたものはないでしょう。**たたき上げ**のこの人物は、自らの土建会社が戦時中の請け負いで成長し、富豪になりました。田中は1947年の国会議員選挙で初当選、自民党が結成されると入党し、政治組織の資金調達を**陰で操る達人**として瞬く間にその地位を築きました。最初の任期中、炭鉱国営化に反対票を投じるよう炭鉱業者から賄賂を

保釈金２億円を払って東京拘置所
から保釈される田中角栄
（1976年）

Scandals and Corruption

The issue of "**money poli-tics**" became especially sensitive in the 1960s and 1970s. It cost huge sums of money to get elected to the National Diet and further sums to provide the care that **home districts** expected from their representatives. Politicians gained loyalty by contributing to local charities, supporting local businesses and sending gifts at weddings and festivals. To support this outlay, they needed significant **intakes of cash**, which often came from wealthy businessmen and companies. It was understood, of course, that such "contributions" would buy favorable consideration of related legislation.

Perhaps no other scandals caught the public eye more than those surrounding Prime Minister Tanaka Kakuei. A **self-made man**, his construction company made him rich from contracts during wartime. Winning his first election to the National Diet in 1947, he joined the LDP after it was formed and quickly established himself as a **master of behind-the-scenes** funding for the political machine. During his first term of office, he was charged with accepting bribes from the coal indus-

得た容疑で逮捕されました。

　彼は最初の再選をかけた選挙に拘置所から立候補しましたが、投票日直前に保釈となりました。彼は自らの選挙区である新潟に深い関心を寄せていたため、有権者は彼を国会の議席に送り返しました。その後、彼は裁判では無罪になっています。

　田中の強力な支持層、「後援会」と呼ばれる地方の支援組織が彼を支えたことは、日本の政治全体に働くある法則を示しています。重要なのは、その政治家が政府に圧力をかけ、いかに金を地元の地域に落とせるかどうかなのです。このことは、しばしば地方の住民の賃金源となる**公共事業**を意味しました。設備が必要か、または環境に有害かどうかなど関係ありません。彼は、高速道路、学校、トンネル、**鉄道建設**、**除雪事業**を公約し、すべて**実現させました**。1983年までに新潟県は、県民1人当たりの公共事業支出額において、47都道府県中トップになりました。その見返りとして、彼は支援者から揺るぎない支持を得ました。

　全国的に見て、田中は高校も卒業していないという点で稀有な存在であり、政治家や官僚がしばしば東京大学の卒業生であるのとは対照的でした。1972年に首相に就任すると、マスメディアはほぼ連日、建設業者や不動産業者からの巨額の献金に関する新たな疑惑を報道しました。1974年、彼はついに辞職に追い込まれましたが、自民党の闇将軍として政界への強い影響力を保ちました。

try to vote against nationalizing the coal mines.

He ran for his first reelection from jail, but managed to get released on bail just before the election. Because he had paid careful attention to his Niigata constituency, voters there returned him to his Diet seat. He later successfully appealed his bribery case.

The fact that Tanaka's staunchest supporters, in a local organization called *koenkai*, stood behind him illustrated the principle at work throughout politics in Japan: what matters is whether the politician succeeds in pressuring the central government to disperse resources to the local region. Often this has meant **public works**—a source of wages for local residents—regardless of whether the facility is necessary or harmful to the environment. He promised highways, schools, tunnels, railroads and **snow-removal services**, and he **delivered**. By 1983 Niigata prefecture was first among the 47 prefectures in terms of per capita expenditures for public works. In return, his supporters offered loyal support.

On the national scene, Tanaka was unique in having never completed high school, in contrast to the politicians and bureaucrats who were often graduates of the University of Tokyo. Once elected prime minister in 1972, the mass media reported almost daily some new allegation of huge contributions to him from the construction business and real estate business. He was finally driven from office in 1974 but remained a power-broker behind the LDP machine.

退陣から2年後、米上院の外交委員会の公聴会で、田中が賄賂として5億円を受け取ったことをロッキード社が証言し、田中は逮捕されました。全日空に、新型の大型ジェット旅客機L1011トライスターを購入するよう「勧めた」見返りに賄賂を得たという容疑でした。この事件で、「**構造汚職**」という言葉が人々の口に上りました。金がここまで政治機構の一部と化したことで、新しい用語まで作られたのです。選挙費用の計算には「実弾」という言葉が使われました。「実弾」1発は1億円でした。やがて辞書には「実弾」の第2の意味として「現金」と記されました。

　何年も裁判と控訴を繰り返した後、田中は最終的に有罪となりましたが、ほぼ致命的な**脳卒中**で倒れ、刑務所行きという事態は免れました。
　野党勢力は自民党からの政権奪取には真剣に挑めなかったものの、こうした汚職に対する世論の怒りはよく代弁しました。中道政党の公明党は、政治汚職の根絶を訴え、さらに**社会福祉制度**の充実を奨励することで支持者を獲得しました。日本共産党は、社会主義政策と再軍備反対に焦点を当てました。日本社会党は、社会主義計画の推進と、米国との軍事協調体制の拡大に反対しました。金権政治の汚職に反対する運動をした人には、1953年に初当選した市川房枝議員もいました。彼女は人権擁護運動の傑出した**代弁者**となりました。

Two years later, he was arrested after a U.S. Senate Foreign Relations Committee hearing into the activities of the Lockheed Aircraft Corporation claimed that he had accepted 500 million yen in bribes from Lockheed. It was alleged that the funds were for "encouraging" the All Nippon Airways to buy new L-1011 TriStar airbuses from Lockheed. The case brought the term *kozo oshoku*, or "**structural corruption**," into the public vocabulary. Money became so much a part of the political machinery that a new jargon was built up around it. The chief way of calculating election expenses was in terms of "*jitsudan*" (bullets)—one "bullet" being ¥100 million. Before long, dictionaries were giving the term a secondary meaning of "money."

After years of trials and appeals, Tanaka was finally found guilty as charged, but a near-fatal **stroke** saved him the embarrassment of actually going to prison.

Although the opposition parties were rarely able to seriously challenge the LDP for national leadership, they often expressed the public outrage at such corruption. The centralist Komeito, Clean Government Party, gained support by calling for the elimination of political corruption, and also for promoting the funding of **social welfare programs**. The Japan Communist Party (JCP) focused its attentions on socialist policies and opposition to rearmament. The Japan Socialist Party (JSP) lobbied for socialist programs and opposed the extension of military affiliation with the United States. Among the independents who campaigned against the corruption

公共事業

　利益誘導型の政治は、1990年代の初めまでに600万以上の雇用を創出した政府出資の大規模建設事業につながりました。この現象は「土建国家」とまで言われ、公共事業の建設現場における被雇用者数は製造業全体のそれを上回っています。さらに、日本の公共事業予算は冷戦期の米国の**国防費**を超えていました。その結果、日本の建設業と政治家の関係は、伝統的に軍需産業と政治家が強い関係にあるとされる米国の状況よりもはるかに強固なものになりました。その**緊密な関係**は税金で成り立つ予算のバラマキの上に築かれており、将

公共事業費の対GDP比率
（2004年）
Ratio of Public Works
Expenditure to GDP
(2004)

＊内閣府データより

	0	1	2	3	4	5 (%)
Japan 日本						4.9%
U.S.A. 米国				3.2%	
U.K. 英国		1.7%			
Germany ドイツ		1.4%			
France フランス				3.3%	

of money politics was Ichikawa Fusae, who first won election to the Diet in 1953 and became a prominent **spokesperson** for human rights.

Public Works

Pork-barrel politics have led to massive government-funded construction projects that by the early 1990s gave work to over six million people. There is even a name for the phenomenon—the construction state (*doken kokka*)—and the number of those employed in construction exceeds the number in the entire manufacturing sector. In addition, Japan's public works budget continued to exceed the U.S. **defense budget** at the height of the Cold War. As a result, the ties between construction enterprises and politicians remains much stronger than, say, the United States, where traditionally the defense industries are believed to have a stronger relationship. The **cozy relationship** is built on the distribution of taxpayers' yen and the huge burden of public works spending will be born by future generations as well.

Japan's media with great regularity uncovers **bid-rigging** for public works contracts (*dango*) and collusion between politicians, bureaucrats, businessmen and the underworld. In early 2006, for example, the current and former officials of the Japan Defense Facilities Administration Agency were investigated for collusion and

来の世代も同様に公共事業支出の大きな負担を負うことになります。

日本のメディアはしばしば、公共事業の**談合**や、政治家、官僚、企業人、ヤクザの癒着を暴いています。2006年の初めにも、防衛施設庁の現職幹部とOBが、防衛庁施設の空調工事の談合をめぐって取り調べを受けました。防衛庁幹部に退職後のポスト——いわゆる「天下り」——を与えた建設会社は、入札前に工事を受注していました。

このような問題に加え、日本では、公共事業は、その事業が本当に必要なものか、または環境問題の見地から妥当であるかどうかにかかわらず、ほとんどいつも失業者を減らす最も容易な方法だと考えられています。

農村の生活

1950年、農村部の人口は総人口の72%を占め、1952年には日本国民のほぼ半数が農業に従事していました。しかし、都市部の仕事や娯楽がより充実すると、農村部から都市部への大規模な人口移動が始まりました。1972年までに、農村部住民は人口のわずか32%に減り、1990年までに、農業従事者数は全労働人口の約5%になりました。

東北の「辺境」や日本海沿岸地域の**過疎化**により、打ち捨てられた廃屋と年寄りだけの

rigging bids for air-conditioning contracts for Defense Agency facilities. Construction firms that had given former agency officials post-retirement positions—known as "descent from heaven" or *amakudari*—were awarded contracts prior to the bidding.

In addition, public work projects are almost invariably seen in Japan as the simplest way to reduce unemployment, regardless of whether the construction project is either necessary or environmentally wise.

長崎県・諫早湾干拓事業の
堤防締め切り工事で次々と
落とされる鋼板。地元の漁
協や自然保護団体の猛反発
にあっている（1997年）

Life on the Farms

In 1950, 72% of the population still lived in rural areas and in 1952 almost half of Japan's population was working in the fields. When jobs and entertainments of the city became more available, however, a mass exodus to the cities began. By 1972, only 38% were still there and by 1990, about 5% of the Japanese workers were still working in the fields.

Depopulation in "remote areas" of Tohoku, northeast Japan, and the coast of the Sea of Japan left small

小さな村々が残りました。家族のなかの若い世代が都市に移り住むと、学校は廃校になり、地元の商店は閉店しました。地元住民が運良く村を維持できると、郵便局が地域社会の活動の中心になりました。

当初、農村地域は生活水準の面で都会に大きく遅れをとっていましたが、植え付けや刈り取りといった農作業の機械化が急速に進み――自民党の後押しで農業補助金制度も導入され――、状況は急速に改善されました。手頃な価格の電動耕作機も、1955年に8万9000台だったのが1970年には350万台に増え、日本は、ほかの農産物はともかく、コメは**自給自足**で賄われています。

田植え、農薬や水の散布、収穫、**脱穀**、輸送の機械化は、農家の生活様式に大きな影響を及ぼしました。男性が日がな一日農作業をする必要もなくなり、しかも農家にはしばしば女性の働き手もありました。農作業の代わりに、男性は、週日や農閑期に、各地域の街で短期やパートタイムの仕事に就いて収入を得ました。農家の女性も、工場のパート労働や店の従業員として働き、家計を支えました。農作業は、就業後や休日にできたのです。正規の職に就き、妻や老人に農作業を任せる男性もいました。こうした現象は「三ちゃん農業」として知られ、日本人が親しみを込めて、妻を「かあちゃん」、祖父を「じいちゃん」、祖母を「ばあちゃん」と呼ぶことからそう呼ばれるようになりました。

hamlets with derelict houses and an aged population. When the younger members of families moved to the cities, the schools and local shops closed up. If the local residents were lucky enough to keep it, the local post office became the center of community activity.

At first, farming communities were considerably behind the urban communities in living standards, but the rapid introduction of mechanical planting and harvesting equipment—and the maintenance of farm subsidies through LDP support—rapidly remedied the situation. Affordable motorized walking tractor-tillers increased in number from 89,000 in 1955 to 3.5 million in 1970, allowing Japan to become **self-sufficient** in rice, if in little other agricultural products.

Mechanization of **crop planting**, spraying, harvesting, **threshing** and transportation had a major impact on farm lifestyles. No longer was it necessary for the men of the family to work full-time in the fields, often with the women alongside. Instead, men found temporary or part-time wage-paying jobs in the regional towns to bring in income during the week or agricultural off-seasons. Even farm women supplemented the family budget by part-time work in factories or as clerks in shops. The farm work could be done after-hours or on days off. Some men went to work full-time and left the farm work entirely to their wives and older people. The phenomenon became known as "*san-chan* farming," a reference to the familiar ending attached to the Japanese for wife (*kaachan*), grandfather (*jiichan*) and grandmother (*baachan*).

しかし、農業の機械化は大規模な失業には結びつきませんでした。若者は農村を出ることができ、また実際に出ていきましたが、年長者が農業を続けることができ、ほかの職業を辞めて農業に戻ることもできました。重要なのは、農業従事者の大半は、家を出て都市に移り住むことはなかったということです。

1960年代には多くの農業従事者が、春から秋の収穫まで農作業をし、冬の間の数カ月間、都市に一時的に移って建設作業の仕事に就くという出稼ぎの繰り返しをしていました。

全体的にいえば、農業の機械化と近代化に**副収入**が組み合わさって、地方の総収入は増えました。実際、1973年までに農家の平均収入は都市家庭の収入より7%多くなりました。

🄰 農業の自給自足

日本の食料自給率は年々低下する傾向にあります。その理由として、兼業農家率の増加や、日本人の食生活の変化などが挙げられますが、注目すべき点として、コメ消費の減少と肉・乳製品消費の増加があります。

日本の食料自給率は、主要国のなかで最低で、カロリーベースの自給率を100とすると、英国74、ドイツ91、フランス130、米国119、オーストラリア230となっているのに対し、日本はわずか40です（2004年度）。

2004年の農林水産省調査によると、主要食物の自給率では、コメ95.2％、小麦13.7％、豆5.9％、野菜80.1％、肉類44％、牛乳・乳製品67.3％となっています。

食料輸入には、政治、安全の両面から制限が加えられることもあります。例えば、ニクソン人統領が大豆の対日輸出を凍結したのは政治的理由によるものでしたし、日本がBSE問題で米国産牛肉の輸入を禁止したのは安全面への配慮によるものでした。日本人は食料輸入規制がいかに深刻な問題であるかを認識せざるを得ないのです。

Farm mechanization did not, however, create a large population of unemployed. While it is true that the young people could and did leave the farms, older farmers were able to stay on, or return to farming after a career in other work. The key element is that the majority of farmers did not leave their homes and move to the cities.

In the 1960s, large numbers of farm workers participated in the *dekasegi* routine of working on the land from spring through harvest in the fall, then moving temporarily to the cities to do construction work through the winter months.

In general the mechanization and modernization of agriculture combined with **supplemental income** raised the total income of the countryside. In fact, the average income of farm families by 1973 was 7% higher than

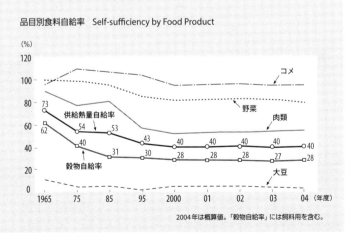

品目別食料自給率　Self-sufficiency by Food Product

2004年は概算値。「穀物自給率」には飼料用を含む。

この数値は1990年までには20%に上がり、農家は都会の人々よりずっと広い敷地に自宅を建て直し、都会の親戚が持っているような現代的な家電もすべて備えていました。

農村部の地域社会が、教育や仕事で都市に一定期間住んだ若者を郷里に取り戻そうと、いわゆる「Uターン」に取り組みましたが、成果は限られたものでした。少数——それでも、現象としては興味深い——が、いわゆる「Iターン」移住者でした。都市出身労働者や退職者は、農村部の生活様式に魅力を感じて移り住んだのです。

女性が便利な都市部に住み、農業より楽な仕事の男性との結婚を望むため、地元の男性が結婚相手を見つけにくく、東北ではいくつかの村の団体が、地元で農業を営む男性とアジア諸国の女性とのお見合いを実験的に行うほどでした。

都市化現象

地理的な特性が日本経済の命運を左右してきたことは、諸外国と比較して考えるとよく分かります。第1に、日本の周囲には大小の良好な港が並び、人口のほとんどは沿岸、または沿岸からやや内陸に集中しています。このため、米国のような広大な国に比べ、国際輸送が極めて効率的です。第2に、山の多い日本の**地形**

the income of urban families. By 1990 that figure rose to 20% above urban families and farmers rebuilt homes with larger space than city dwellers installing all the modern appliances of their city relatives.

Attempts by rural communities to entice young people to return to their native places after a period in the cities pursuing education or working—in the so-called "U-turn" pattern—met with limited success. Small in number—but interesting as a phenomenon— were the so-called "I-turn" migrants. These city-born workers and retirees moved to the country because they found the lifestyle more appealing.

Because women preferred to marry men in cities with more conveniences and less work than on the farm and local farmers were having difficulty finding mates, a few Tohoku village organizations even experimented with matchmaking arrangements for local farming men and women from other Asian nations.

Urbanization

Geographical features have affected Japan's economic fortunes in ways that can only be seen by comparing it with other nations. First, Japan is lined with good harbors, large and small, and its population resides mostly along the coast or within a short distance of the coast. Because of this, international transportation is highly efficient, compared to broad, spacious countries like

から、**可住地**の約30%に住民が住まざるをえないことです。国連の世界人口推計2003年版によると、日本の人口密度は1平方キロメートル当たり336人でした。これは韓国（473人）、オランダ（389人）に次ぐ世界第3位でした。英国（240人）、ドイツ（231人）、米国（30人）と比較しても、日本は極めて込み合ったストレスの多い環境になっています。

しかし、人口密度が格段に高いことから、高速道路、鉄道、地下鉄、送電線、街路、**下水道**などのインフラは、相対的に多くの人のために機能できます。言い換えれば、郵便配達人、警察官、消防士、バス運転手、配送人は、米国、カナダ、オーストラリアなど国よりも多くの人にサービスを提供できます。これらの国々では、広大な**平地**が都市のスプロール現象（無秩序な開発化）と、インフラ、サービス両面の非効率をもたらしました。

🐻 クマの襲撃

2004年はほぼ毎日、ツキノワグマが日本のどこかで民家や事務所、工場、果樹園に侵入した年でした。例えば広島県では、68歳の農夫が台所のドアを引っ掻く音を聞いてドアを開けたところ、クマを見つけてしまいました。クマはすかさず家に入り込むと、廊下で眠ってしまいました。その後捕獲されたクマは、やせ衰えて、体重はわずか47.5キロしかありませんでした。

人口密集地でクマの出没が突然増えたことは、1950年代以降の日本の農村部における経済的、人口統計的変化に関する多くのことを明らかにしています。輸入木材の人気が高まり、国内産の木材がほとんど売れなくなったために、植林された森林が野放しにされて荒廃する一方、クマなどの野生動物の数が

the United States. Second, Japan's mountainous **terrain** forces the population to settle in the small percent (about 30%) of **inhabitable land**. According to the 2003 United Nations World Population Prospects, Japan had 336 people per square kilometer. It ranked third behind South Korea (473) and the Netherlands (389). Compared with the U.K. (240), Germany (231) and the United States (30), it is extremely crowded, leading to a stressful environment.

However, as a result of that exceptional density, highways, railroads, subways, electric power lines, streets, **sewers** and other forms of infrastructure are able to serve more people. In turn, service provided by mail carriers, police officers, fire fighters, bus drivers and delivery personnel can reach far more people than the same services in areas like the U.S., Canada and Australia. In these nations, abundant **flat land** has led to greater urban sprawl and less efficiency in both infrastructure and services.

増えています。かつて地元住民が木炭を作ったり、薪を集めに行っていた山村周辺の森林地帯は、人とクマを隔てる緩衝地帯の役割を果たしていました。

しかし、こうした地域の住民が急激に減少し、高齢者の家庭がわずかに残るだけになりました。しばしば人が出入りしていた森林地帯は廃れ、クマを遠ざけていた緩衝地帯がなくなりました。クマが食べるドングリの木が台風でなぎ倒されると、クマは畑の農作物や人家の生ゴミを求めて山から下りてくるのです。2004年もこうした要素が重なったことから、地方でクマに遭遇するケースが頻繁に生じました。

また、この人口密度の高さは、部品の輸送システム「ジャスト・イン・タイム」のような革新的制度ももたらしたといえます。家電やオーディオの**小型化**にも貢献したかも知れません。

サラリーマンと専業主婦

農業、漁業、森林業の労働者が農村部での仕事を捨てて都市部に移り住み、製造業などで安定賃金を得るようになると、教育のある都市生活者は給与制の事務職の口を大企業に求めるようになりました。「サラリーマン」と呼ばれるようになったこれらの人々は、いわゆる「新中間層」を象徴していました。会社に忠誠を尽くし、日常的に残業し、休暇はほとんど取らず、退社後も同僚や取引先との飲み会に参加するこれらの「会社員」は出世の階段を上りました。企業が大手であれば給料は上がり、**年功序列**によって昇進し、いったん就職すれば定年まで同じ会社で働くことをあてにできました。

1980年代にサラリーマンが過度の勤労意欲を要求されるようになると、過労による死、「**過労死**」が、その現象を表す言葉となりました。1日12〜16時間、週6〜7日の労働は当たり前になりました。だれもが遅くまで残業し、

過労死
" karoshi " は日本独自の言葉で、" tsunami " などの日本語と同じように英語など他言語の辞書にもそのまま掲載されています。過労死とは、長時間労働などによる極度の精神的、肉体的負担で働き盛りの会社員が突然死することですが、日本以外にこの事柄に該当する言葉がないからです。この言葉は日本人の会社員を象徴する言葉として広まっているのです。

One can also make the case that this high density has driven innovations such the "just-in-time" system of the delivery of parts to factories. It may also have contributed to the **miniaturization** of household appliances and audio equipment.

Emergence of the *Sarariiman* and Full-time Housewife

As more farmers, fishermen and foresters gave up their jobs in rural areas to move to urban areas where they could find manufacturing jobs which paid steady wages, the more educated urban-dwellers aimed for jobs as salaried, white-collar office workers for large firms. These "*sarariiman*," as they came to be called, symbolized what was called a "New Middle Class." Totally devoted to their companies, working overtime routinely, rarely taking vacations and joining colleagues and clients for drinks in the off-hours, these "company men" climbed the corporate ladder to success. In the larger corporations, their salaries went up and they were promoted in **lock-step order by age** (*nenko joretsu*) and they counted on working at the same company from first employment until retirement.

The excesses of the work ethic required of salaried workers became obvious in the 1980s and a word was coined to describe the phenomenon: *karoshi*, **death from over work**. Six and seven-day weeks of 12 to 16 hours began to take their toll. In an environment where

休日に出勤する人もいる職場環境では、それ
も特異ではなかったかもしれません。しかし、
1990年より以前、日本の会社員は欧米の会社
員に比べ、年間200〜300時間も多く働いてい
ました。これに1時間半〜2時間の通勤時間が
加わり、家ではほとんど寝るだけでした。やが
て、年間1万人もの日本人が純粋に過労で死に
至っていると推計されました。

　そのようなサラリーマンと結婚した女性は、
労働の必要性からは解放されました。そのかわ
り、彼女たちは旧世代の「良妻賢母」のよう
に、快適な家庭環境を作り、家族に仕えるもの
とされました。妻は何よりもまず、子どもを養
育し、マンションや小さな一戸建てを守り、買
い物などの家事を引き受けました。旧世代の
既婚女性よりも、経済的に安定し、自由な時間
を多く享有できるようになりましたが、多くの
女性はいつも家を空ける夫に不満を抱き、日々
の家事に退屈を感じました。

　旧世代の子どもは教育を終えるとすぐに家
業を継ぐものでしたが、サラリーマンという
新たな階層の子どもはそうではありませんで
した。男子は高校で懸命に勉強して少しでも
上位の大学に入学することが期待されました。
上位の大学に入れなかった者は、予備校で1
年以上浪人し、翌年の大学入試に備えました。
女子は、短大に2年間通い、OLつまり「オフィ
ス・レディ」として単調な事務的、秘書的な仕
事を数年務め、その間に日本の伝統的芸能の

everyone worked late and some also came in on days off, it may not have seemed unusual. But prior to 1990, Japanese business people were putting in 200 to 300 more hours per year than their counterparts in the West. Add to this a 90–120 minute commute to the office, and hours at home were mostly spent sleeping. Before long, it was estimated that as many as 10,000 Japanese were simply working themselves to death each year.

Women who married such white-collar workers were freed from the necessity of working. Instead they were expected to provide a comfortable home environment and serve their family, like the "good wife, wise mother" of earlier generations. The wife was primarily responsible for raising the children, maintaining their condominium (*manshon*) or small house, shopping and otherwise managing the **household**. While these women enjoyed greater financial security and more free time than married women of earlier generations, many felt frustration with their husbands who were always absent and felt bored with the routines of housekeeping.

Children of earlier generations had been expected to succeed to the family business upon completing their education, but children of the new class of white-collar workers did not face that possibility. Instead, boys were expected to study hard enough in high school to gain entrance to a relatively high-ranking university. Those who did not gain entrance to high-ranking university spent an extra year or more in **cram schools** to prepare for the following year's university entrance exams. Expectations of girls were that they would study

習い事をして、父と同じようなサラリーマンと結婚するものと考えられました。長男とは結婚しないのが理想でした。同居する姑のいいなりになるからでした。

中流日本

1973年の「オイルショック」は、日本人の「経済的奇跡」にとってスピード抑止帯となりました。年間の経済成長率が10%という力強さは影を潜めました。急成長に慣れていた日本人には、このことが大きな**後退**のように思えました。しかし、諸外国には、1975年から1980年代の日本のGNP成長率3.5〜5.5%は実に羨むべきものと映りました。日本の経済発展が非の打ちどころのない水準に達したの

🍴 食生活の変化

終戦直後、日本人は1500キロカロリー以下という必要最低限カロリーも摂取できませんでしたが、1980年代後半までには約2600キロカロリーを摂るようになりました。その上、コメ、野菜、魚中心の食生活だったのが、肉、果物、乳製品を多く食べるようになりました。若い世代は、食べるコメの量が減ったことから炭水化物摂取量が減り、タンパク質摂取量が増えました。2003年までに若者の身長は祖父母の世代より男女とも5センチ以上伸びました。

for two years in a junior college, spend a few years doing menial administrative and clerical work as an "OL" or "office lady" while taking lessons in Japanese traditional arts on the side and then settle down with a white-collar husband like her father. Ideally, she would not marry an elder son, because if she did, she would be under the thumb of her live-in mother-in-law.

Middle-class Japan

The "oil shock" of 1973 acted as a speed bump for the Japanese "economic miracle." The dynamic 10% annual growth of the economy ended. To those Japanese who had grown accustomed to rapid growth, this seemed a major **retreat**. But to the outside world, Japan's 3.5% to 5.5% growth in GNP during the years from 1975 through the 1980s seemed quite enviable. An undeniable benchmark of progress was reached in 1987 when Japan's per capita GNP surpassed that of the U.S.

True enough, because there is only limited land available for housing, Japanese housing is more cramped than that of Europe and the U.S. However, by most other standards, by the early 1970s the urban standard of living in Japan rivaled that of other advanced nations.

The economic recovery and increasing affluence of Japan were widely recognized by foreign observers, including sociologist Ezra Vogel, whose *Japan as Number One: Lessons for America* became a bestseller in

は、1987年に1人当たりGNPが米国を上回ったときのことです。

　実際、住宅地向けの土地が限られているため、日本の住宅は欧米よりもかなり窮屈です。しかしそれ以外の点では、1970年代初めまでに日本の都市生活水準はほかの先進諸国に匹敵するようになりました。

　日本の経済復興と豊かさの増大は、日米両国のベストセラー『ジャパン・アズ・ナンバーワン』を著した社会学者エズラ・ヴォーゲルなど海外の専門家に広く認知されました。ヴォーゲルはこの書物で、日本の経済的活力は、様々な問題はあっても、ほかのどの国よりも平等主義の社会に導いたと結論づけました。例えば、日本では高所得世帯の上位20%の平均月収は、低所得世帯の下位20%の平均月収の約3倍でした。国際的な基準からすると——特に米国と比較すると——この格差は小さなものです。ヴォーゲルの主張を裏付ける事実は、市民自らの経済的位置に関する各種調査にも見られました。

　そのなかでも、総理府が毎年実施した「国民生活調査」は、「ほかの人と比べてあなたの生活レベルは、下、中の下、中、中の上、上のどれだと思いますか？」という質問を毎年行っています。1970代、1980年代は、自らの生活レベルを「中」とした人の割合が着実に増え、60%を超えました。「中の下」「中の上」の回答を加えると、「中」と位置づけた人は90%を優に超えました。

America and in Japan. Vogel concluded in this volume that despite its various problems Japan's economic dynamism had led to a more egalitarian society than any other nation. As an example, the gap between the average monthly income of the top 20% of households was roughly three times that of the average for the bottom 20%. By international standards—and particularly compared with the U.S.—this was a small gap. Evidence for Vogel's claim was also found in various surveys of the populace as to where they placed themselves economically.

Among these, the Prime Minister's Office (*Sorifu*) in its annual "Opinion Survey of the People's Livelihood" (*Kokumin seikatsu chosa*) each year asked, "Compared to other people, how do you view your own standard of living? Do you think of your own position as lower, lower-middle, middle-middle, upper-middle or upper?" The percentage of those who placed themselves in the "middle-middle" category steadily increased during the 1970s and 1980s until it reached more than 60%. If the

🏥 国民皆保険

　日本では、国民皆保険制度によって医療費が低額に抑えられてきたため、日本人は最近まで、軽症でも進んで病院で診察を受けてきました。米国人が年平均5回病院で診察するのに対し、日本人は年平均15回病院の治療を受けます。健康保険で医療費が支払われるため、多くの場合、患者は医療費の3割を負担するだけで、市販の薬で十分間に合う風邪でも、信頼できる病院や専門医の治療を受けられます。老齢の患者にとって病院通いは社交でもあり、仲間同士が定期的に集まって待合室でお喋りに興じるのです。その結果、日本では「3時間待って診察5分」ということも珍しくありません。

地方と中心部大都市、農村部と都会の文化的格差も解消されたように思われました。同じファッション、音楽、ファーストフードが全国どこでも手に入ります。全国どこでも、各学年の子どもはほかの地域と事実上同じ授業を受けました。例えば、郵政省が、歌の最初の1小節とイラストがデザインされた歌シリーズの切手を発行していたと聞けば、米国人は驚くでしょう。日本の学童は各学年で同じ歌を学びますが、米国では州・市が、各学年で教える歌を独自に選ぶことになっています。**全国放送**や全国紙はすべての人に同じニュースを送りました。後者の新聞は米国と対照的です。米国の大新聞は、一部のビジネス紙と『USAトゥデー』以外、主に各地域の読者を想定した地方紙なのです。

　また、日本人は自らを「働きバチ」だと思いがちですが、少なくとも1970年代後半以降の国際比較によれば、日本人は決して例外的ではありません。1979年に余暇開発センターは

日本人の体格の変化
（20 〜 24歳の平均値）
Japanese Average
Physical Stature at
Age 20–24

*文部科学省データより

年 Year	男 Male		女 Female	
	身長 Height	体重 Weight	身長 Height	体重 Weight
1900	160.9 cm	53.0 kg	147.9 cm	48.0 kg
1945	165.0	57.3	153.2	51.2
1955	165.5	56.0	154.3	49.9
1965	167.5	58.2	155.4	50.8
1977	169.4	60.5	156.7	50.6
1985	170.6	63.4	157.7	50.6
1995	171.1	64.1	158.4	51.2
2000	171.8	65.4	158.4	50.3
2010	171.8	65.8	158.8	50.8
2015	171.8	65.7	158.3	50.4
2020	171.5	65.4	157.8	49.6
2022	171.5	65.2	157.8	50.7

lower-middle and upper-middle respondents are added, the figure in the self-defined "middle" group rose well above 90%.

The cultural gap between the regions and central metropolises and between rural and urban communities seemed to disappearing. The same clothing fashions, music and fast foods were available in every part of the country. Across the nation children in each school grade was studying virtually the same lessons as their counterparts in other parts of the country. It would be surprising to an American, for example, to hear that the Japanese postal service issued a series of stamps based on songs, each with the first bars of the music and an illustrative design. Where every Japanese schoolchild learns the same songs in the same grade, in America each state and even city may have its own selection of songs to be taught in each grade. **National broadcasting** and national newspapers brought the same news to everyone. The latter point marked a contrast with the U.S., where with the exception of business newspapers and USA *Today*, the major newspapers are produced primarily for a regional readership.

Although the Japanese tend to think of themselves as work-oriented "worker bees" (*hataraki bachi*), international comparisons from at least the late 1970s have shown that they are by no means exceptional. In 1979, the Leisure Development Center surveyed people in 13 nations on values and asked whether they found fulfillment primarily in work, leisure or family. Work placed on top in Japan (40%), but the Japanese were lower

13カ国の人々を対象に価値観の調査を行い、仕事、余暇、家庭のどれに最も充足感を感じるかという質問を行いました。日本では仕事と答えた人がトップでしたが（40%）、イタリア人（44%）、ドイツ人（42%）、英国人（42%）よりも低い比率でした。

「リッチ・ジャパニーズ」

1980年代後半、高価なカメラを持ち、最新のファッションに身を包んだ日本人観光客が至る所に現れたとき、実際、諸外国が恐れを抱いたとは言わないまでも、羨望の目で見ていました。ニューヨークのロックフェラーセンター、ハリウッド映画会社や国際的な名画が日本人の手に落ちると、諸外国の人々は、日本人が世界を乗っ取るのではと思い始めました。1987年にゴッホの作品が史上最高の4000万ドルで落札されたことは、日本人にほとんど何でもできる**財力**があることを世界に示しました。

🎧 ディスコ・フィーバー

1991年、防衛大学校のある卒業生が「ジュリアナ東京」をプロデュースしたことで一躍有名になりました。バブル期の若者は、夜になると「お立ち台」を備えた六本木のディスコに繰り出しました。昼間は典型的なOLが、夜には変身しました。露出度の高いミニスカートに着替えると、彼女たちはダンスフロアで羽根つき扇子を振り回しながら踊り、色目使いで見上げる

than the Italians (44%), Germans (42%) and the British (41%).

"Rich Japanese"

In fact, other nations watched enviously, if not alarmed, when in the late 1980s Japanese tourists appeared everywhere, carrying expensive cameras and wearing the latest fashions. When New York's Rockefeller Center, Hollywood studios and international-class works of art came into Japanese hands, citizens of other countries began wondering whether the Japanese might take over the world. The purchase of a Van Gogh painting for a record $40 million in 1987 suggested to the world that the Japanese had the **financial clout** to do almost anything.

男性たちを喜ばせました。ディスコは、日本のバブル経済を象徴する社会現象にもなったのです。しかし、いったんバブルがはじけてしまうと、六本木にも不景気が訪れました。皮肉にも、流行の「ジュリアナ東京」のプロデューサーは、1997年から人材派遣、ヘルスケア、介護ビジネスに乗り出しました。

着物を着た「自由の女神」
を表紙にあしらいソニーの
旧コロンビア映画買収を大
きく報じた Newsweek
（1988年）

　新たに出現した若い富裕層の文化を象徴的
に描いたのが、大学生の田中康夫が書いた小説
『なんとなくクリスタル』（1981年）でした。そ
の後、長野県知事となった田中は、この作品で
消費志向の強い都会の若者たちを捉えました。
彼らの生活は、青山のお洒落なブティックや深
夜の六本木でのパーティーを中心にまわり、ほ
かのことにはほとんど関心がないようでした。

　日本人の大半は、1980年代までに経済的に
は成功を収めたと考えたでしょうが、多くの
人にとって、その発展には重い社会的犠牲も
ありました。都市の就労者はますます長時間
となる通勤と労働に直面していました。多く
の人にとって、住居は相変わらず高くて狭く、
あるヨーロッパ人訪問客が言ったように「ウ
サギ小屋」のようでした。

　裕福な人々とまったく対照的だったのが、
定職のない炭鉱夫や**日雇い労働者**からなる**社
会離脱層**とホームレス、さまざまな農民、生活
保護者、精神的に病む人でした。いわゆる高度
経済成長は、明らかにすべての人のプラスと
いうわけではなかったのです。

ノスタルジー

　岡本太郎の「太陽の塔」や、月の石を揃えた
大阪万博には6400万人が訪れ、日本が世界に
おいて堅固な経済的地位を占めたことをその

Symbolic of the newly rich youth culture was university student Tanaka Yasuo's "Somehow or other, crystal" (*Nantonaku kurisutaru*, 1981). Tanaka, who later became governor of Nagano prefecture, captured in this work the **consumption-oriented** urban young crowd. Their lives seemed to revolve around fashionable Aoyama boutiques, late night partying at discos in Roppongi and little concern for others.

Most Japanese would have admitted that Japan had achieved economic success by the 1980s, but for many, there were heavy social costs for that improvement. Urban workers faced increasingly longer commutes to their workplaces and longer work hours. For many, housing remained expensive and cramped, like "rabbit hutches," as one European visitor commented.

In strict contrast to the very rich was a group of **castoffs** and homeless, composed of former miners, **day laborers** who could not find jobs and assorted farmers, welfare cases and mentally unstable. The so-called high-speed economic growth clearly did not benefit everyone.

Nostalgia

The Osaka Expo, complete with Okamoto Taro's Sun Symbol and "moon rocks," hosted 64 million visitors who came to confirm that Japan now had a solid

大阪万博。太陽の塔と広場
に集まる人々
（1970年）

目で確かめるとともに、輝かしい未来世界の一端を見ました。しかし万博が閉会した直後、10月には日本国有鉄道——現在のJRの前身——が、理想化された過去を求める象徴的キャンペーン「ディスカバー・ジャパン」を展開しました。日本の歴史上最も長く続いたキャンペーンの一つで、その基調をなすモットーは「日本の豊かな自然、美しい歴史や伝統、こまやかな人情を、旅によって発見し、自分のものにしよう」でした。

忘れられかけた、より日本らしい日本に出会う都会の若者——多くは女性——を主役にすえたキャンペーンのCMやポスターは、日本人であることの意味をまさに再発見する方法として、嬬恋や倉敷といった都会から離れた風景のなかで伝統的な仕事に従事する人々との出会いを取り上げました。それは、ある意味で、残されている伝統が失われる前に見つけておこうと日本人に訴えるキャンペーンでした。日本が急速に発展し、もはや伝統に根ざしてはいないことは、1984年に展開された新たな観光キャンペーン「エキゾチック・ジャパン」で明らかになりました。このときには、伝統的な日本は「異質」で「外来」のものになっていたのです。

もう一つの例は、演歌歌手・千昌夫の『北国の春』が人気を博したことです。演歌は伝統的に故郷や失った恋の感傷に浸るものでしたが、邦楽、洋楽ともにほかのジャンルの人気が高まったために、演歌は次第に低迷していまし

economic place in the world and to glimpse the bright future world. But as soon as Expo closed, in October Japan National Railway—precursor to today's Japan Railway (JR)—launched "Discover Japan," an emblematic campaign to promote the idealized past. One of the longest-running campaigns in Japanese history, the campaign's underlying motto was "Discover through travel Japan's bountiful nature, beautiful history and tradition, and delicate human feelings, and make them your own."

Featuring young—usually female—urbanites encountering a more authentic, mostly forgotten Japan, the commercials and posters for the campaign offered encounters with traditionally employed people in remote landscapes, such as Tsumagoi and Kurashiki. It was presented as a way to rediscover exactly what it means to be Japanese. In a way, it was a campaign urging Japanese to discover what remained of tradition before it was lost. That Japan had progressed rapidly and was no longer rooted in tradition was underlined by the new tourism slogan introduced in 1984: "Exotic Japan." By this time, traditional Japan had become "**foreign**" and "**non-native**."

Another example of this was the popularity of *enka* singer Sen Masao's song *Kitaguni no haru. Enka* traditionally waxed nostalgic for the old home place and for lost love, but with the rise in popularity of other forms, both Japanese and western, the audience for *enka* had

た。しかし、この曲は違っていました。1977年に発売されると、翌78年に次第に人気が上がり、結果的には300万枚以上を売り上げ、ほかのアジア諸国でも流行しました。地方に住む母が歌手になった都会の息子に季節の移り変わりを伝えようと小包を送るものの、息子はそれすら気づかないという状況を、ほろ苦い歌詞で熱情的に歌いあげました。息子は、地方に残してきた恋人や、しばしば一緒に酒を酌み交わしているだろう父や弟の姿を思い出します。そして、何よりも大事なことに、息子は「あのふるさとへ帰ろかな」と思いまどうのです。

この曲のなかの「ふるさと」は現実よりも理想的で、その歌手は、便利で刺激的で、定収入を得られる仕事のある都会にとどまるでしょう。レコードを買った人々も同じです。しかし、この曲が非常に幅広く流行したことは、便利な都会の生活が完全に充足的なものではないことを示すようでした。おそらく何か精神的なものが失われてしまったのです。経済的成功、賃金上昇、便利な生活様式は、より温かい人間関係や、より素朴な真の喜びを犠牲にして得られたのかもしれません。

都会で生活する孤独な地方出身者の目にどのように映ったかはともかく、現実に光を当てれば、地方の**僻地**が、不景気、上昇する失業率、**失望と孤立**にますます直面していることは明らかでした。冬の農閑期には農民が仕事と現金収入を求めて工場や橋、道路、ビルの建設現場で仕事をするために都市部に出かけまし

gradually declined. But this song was different. Released in 1977, it grew in popularity in 1978 and eventually sold over three million copies, eventually becoming popular in other Asian nations as well. The bittersweet lyrics rhapsodized about how the singer's mother back in the countryside has sent a small package to the singer with something to remind him of the change of seasons he would not recognize in the city. He remembers the girl he left behind and his own brother and father who are probably sharing a drink on occasion. Most importantly he wonders, *ano furusato e kaerokana*, "maybe I'll go back to the old home."

The "furusato" of the song is more ideal than real, and the singer will undoubtedly remain in the city with its conveniences, excitements and wage-paying jobs, just like those who bought the record. But the broader than usual popularity of the song seemed to indicate that convenient urban life was not entirely satisfying. Perhaps something spiritual had been lost. Economic success, rise in wages and convenient lifestyle had perhaps been purchased at the expense of warmer relationships and simpler real pleasures.

Regardless of how it seemed from the point of view of a lonely migrant in the city, by the light of day it was clear that the **remote areas** (*hekichi*) of the country were increasingly facing economic recession, rising unemployment, **discouragement** and **isolation**. In search of jobs and cash income, farmers departed for the urban areas during the agricultural off-months in winter

た（出稼ぎ）。そのまま二度と帰って来ない人もいました。1945年には日本人の45%を占めた農業従事者は、1984年までにはわずか5.4%に落ち込みました。

　日本の現在と過去を広く見直そうという動きの兆候は、多くの雑誌、書籍、テレビ番組が、「日本人」である意味を問う、いわゆる「日本人論」として知られた議論を取り上げたことに見て取れました。日本人論を著した日本人研究者の大半は、日本人の「独自性」を強調しました。彼らは日本人の脳の違いや（角田忠信）、腸の長さの違い、日本人とユダヤ人の類似性（山本七平がイザヤ・ベンダサンというペンネームで著した『日本人とユダヤ人』1970年）を指摘しました。日本人でない者にとって、このような論説は、非日本人が日本を理解する方法としては噴飯ものでした。単一民族的特性を示そうとするあまり、アイヌ、沖縄人、長期在住のコリアンや中国人、帰国した日系移民子弟が持つ様々な文化も無視していました。

　日本社会をより本格的に調査したものとしては、精神分析医・土居健郎の『甘えの構造』（1971年）や、文化人類学者・中根千枝の『タテ社会の人間関係』（1967年）がありました。これらの論考は、日本人が世界の民族のなかで特にユニークだという自己満足にとどまらなかったこともあって、真摯な研究者の間で相応の評価を得ました。

(*dekasegi*) to take jobs in factories or in constructing bridges, roads and buildings. Some never returned. Where 45% of all Japanese were farmers in 1945, by 1984 that figure had dropped to a mere 5.4%.

Evidence for a broad reexamination of the past and present was a plethora of magazine articles, books and TV programs dealing with what has come to be known as *Nihonjinron*, discussions about what it means to be "Japanese." Many of the Japanese scholars who produced *Nihonjinron* literature emphasize the "uniqueness" of Japanese. They pointed to the difference in the Japanese brain (Tsunoda Tadanobu), the difference in length of the intestine, similarities between the Japanese and the Jews (*Nihonjin to Yudayajin* by Yamamoto Shichihei, under the pen-name of Isaiah BenDasan, 1970) or a more general cultural difference. To non-Japanese, this literature often bordered on the **ridiculous** as a way of understanding Japan. It also ignored the different cultures of the Ainu population, Okinawans, long-resident Koreans and Chinese and **repatriated** descendants of Japanese emigrants in attempting to create a single national character.

Among the more serious examinations of Japanese society were the works of psychoanalyst Doi Takeo, *Anatomy of Dependence* (*Amae no kozo*, 1971), and anthropologist Nakane Chie, *Japanese Society* (*Tateshakai no ningen kankei*, 1967). These latter works gained considerable respect among serious students of Japan at least in part because they did not contend that the Japanese were completely unique among peoples of the world.

外国人労働者

1980年代のバブル期における労働力不足により、「3K労働」(汚い、危険、きつい)の現場で外国人労働者が目立つようになりました。「3K」は、英語では「3D」(dirty, dangerous, difficult)となります。以前は、韓国人と中国人が外国人集団としては最大規模のものでしたが、バブル期には日系ブラジル人、イラン人、マレーシア人、パキスタン人の数も増えました。

当時発表された国連の報告書では、日本が現在の水準の**労働人口**を維持するには年間約60万人の移民受け入れが必要になるだろうと指摘されました。そうなると、日本は2050年までに1700万人の外国人を受け入れることになりますが、日本人が望まない、あるいは日本人にできない労働を移民にさせることができても、日本政府がこれほどの外国人を受け入れることは考えられません。

政治の転換

1980年代中盤まで、自民党の後押しにより立法から直接的に利益を享受した選挙区は、党指導部による金銭スキャンダルや**政治的失態**が相次いでも同党を支持し続けました。しかし、自民党議員が国の**福祉向上**よりも自ら

Immigrant Labor

Labor shortages during the bubble period of the 1980s led to a rise in the use of immigrant labor to perform the "three-*k* jobs" (*kitanai, kiken, kitsui*), or in English, the "three-*d* jobs" (dirty, dangerous, difficult). The Koreans and Chinese were the largest groups of immigrants, but in this period Japanese-Brazilians (265,000 in 2001), Iranians, Malaysians and Pakistanis began to increase in number as well.

A UN report at the time suggested that in order to maintain the current level of the **working population** it would be necessary to accept some 600,000 immigrants per year. That would mean a total of 17 million by the year 2050. Despite the advantages of having immigrants take on jobs which the Japanese either do not want to do or cannot do because of the declining population, it seems unlikely that the government will actively pursue this proposal.

Political Shift

Until the mid-1980s those constituencies that benefited directly from legislation supported by the LDP continued to support the party regardless of the increasingly frequent money scandals and **political gaffes** of the party leaders. But an increasing percentage of the

NTT, JT, JRの誕生
1985年、日本電信電話公社が日本電信電話株式会社、日本専売公社が日本たばこ産業株式会社になり、1987年には日本国有鉄道がJRグループ各社になりました。この三大公社の民営化を上回る規模の郵政民営化が、小泉内閣によって行われました。郵政民営化関連法案が2005年8月8日に国会で否決されると、小泉首相は衆議院を解散しました（郵政解散）。
9月11日の選挙では、郵政民営化賛成派の自民党が圧勝し、10月14日に法案が可決されました。また、日本道路公団の民営化は、一足先の2006年6月に決まっていました。

の利益に関心を抱いているように見えると、自民党に機械的に票を投じることに反発を覚える有権者の比率が高まりました。このように自民党離れした有権者は、国の問題に現実的解決策を提示できない少数派政党を支持するのではなく、むしろ投票そのものをしなくなりました。その結果、国民の熱烈な支持が弱まったにもかかわらず、自民党は政治的な力を維持しました。

1982年に初めて三つの大手公社の**民営化**が提起されたことは、ここで特筆に値するでしょう。

1990年という境界線

1980年代から1990年代への移行期、日本人が明仁の天皇即位（1990年）やサッカー・Jリーグの創設（1991年）に沸いていた一方で、**世界の秩序**は急速な転換を遂げました。38年に及んだ自民党による保守支配の日本政治、いわゆる「55年体制」が終わり、非自民の8政党の連立政権で細川護熙が首相に就任しました。

国際情勢では、1989年に中国で民主化を求めるデモ参加者が、天安門広場で容赦なく鎮圧されました。ソ連では、ゴルバチョフによる「ペレストロイカ」計画のもとで急激な変化が生じました。このソビエト体制の再編と東欧の改革は、最終的にヨーロッパ全体の変化に結びつき

東ドイツ国境警備隊がブランデンブルク門の上で見守る中でベルリンの壁をハンマーで打ち砕くデモ隊（1989年11月）

electorate became unwilling to automatically vote for the LDP when it seemed to them that the party politicians were more concerned about personal advantages than the **betterment of the welfare** of the nation. These alienated voters simply stopped voting rather than vote for minority parties who offered no realistic solution to the real problems that the nation faced. As a result, the LDP maintained its hold on political power, although with less enthusiastic support from the public.

It is worth noting here that in 1982 it was first proposed to **privatize** the three major public corporations.

The Dividing Line of 1990

As the 1980s gave way to the 1990s, while the Japanese were being entertained by the enthronement of Emperor Akihito (1990) and the founding of the J League (1991), the **world order** was rapidly shifting. The 38-year conservative domination Japanese politics by the LDP, under the so-called "system of 1955," came to an end when Hosokawa Morihiro became prime minister with a coalition of eight non-LDP political parties.

On the international scene, in 1989 demonstrators calling for democratization in China were brutally suppressed in the **Tiananmen Square** Incident. Radical change in the Soviet Union began under Gorbachev's program of "perestroika." Eventually this restructuring of the Soviet Union and reforms in Eastern Europe led

ました。1989年、地中海のマルタ島で米ソ首脳が会談し、冷戦終結を公式に宣言しました。1961年から立ちはだかっていた**ベルリンの壁**は1989年に崩壊し、翌年には東西ドイツが再統一されました。ペルシャ湾では、1990年にイラクがクウェートを侵攻し、その翌年には欧米の多国籍軍にイラクが敗れました。1991年にはソ連が解体し、様々な地域がロシア連邦とそのほかの共和国などに再編されました。

国際社会での動き

　日本経済が力を増し、米国の経済的優位を脅かすようにまでなると、米国は軍事同盟においてより大きな役割を日本に求めるようになりました。1990年から1991年の**湾岸戦争**で、この問題は転機を迎えました。

　日本の**世論**と憲法は、イラクのクウェート侵攻を阻止するために送られた多国籍軍の支援のために自衛隊を派遣することを容認しませんでした。しかし、米国は何らかの方法で日本に協力するよう迫りました。長い議論の末、日本政府は軍事費として約130億ドルの支援を決定しました。

　しかし、日米両国ともこの貢献の結果に満足しませんでした。日本人は、多大な貢献——湾岸地域以外の国では最高——が**正当に評価されなかった**と感じました。多くの米国人は、

to changes in Europe as well. The leaders of the U.S. and the U.S.S.R. met at Malta to declare in 1989 that the Cold War was officially over. The **Berlin Wall,** which had stood since 1961, was demolished in 1989 and the following year the two Germanys were reunified. In the Persian Gulf, Iraq invaded Kuwait in 1990 and was defeated the following year by Western forces. In 1991 the Soviet Union dissolved, and a new union was formed by Russia and some of the other republics.

International Events

As Japan's economy strengthened and even challenged American economic dominance, the U.S. began to pressure Japan to play a more active role in their military alliance. This issue came to a turning point during the events of the **Persian Gulf War** of 1990–1991.

Japanese **public opinion** and the Constitution ruled out the dispatching of SDF troops to join the multination expedition sent to resist the Iraqi invasion of Kuwait. However, the U.S. pressured Japan to support the effort in some way. After prolonged debate, the Japanese government contributed some thirteen billion dollars toward the cost of the operation.

Neither side was entirely satisfied with the result of this contribution. The Japanese felt that their major contribution—more than any other nation outside the Persian Gulf region—was **underappreciated.**

自国の石油供給を守るために米軍に頼る日本人を身勝手だと感じていました。日本は石油の半分以上を湾岸諸国から輸入しており、彼らの言い分は、日本は軍を派遣して戦争に参加し、日本人も米国人と同様に生命をかけるべきだというものでした。日本政府は防衛費の上限はGNPの1%でした。例えば1992年では、国民一人当たり約275ドルの負担でした。米国は同年、GNPの5%を防衛費に充てており、国民一人当たり1122ドルの負担になりました。米国人から見ると、日本が軍事費の負担を増やすのは極めて当然でした。

国内で激しい議論が行われ、ようやく1992年に、PKO協力法（国際連合平和維持活動等に対する協力に関する法律）が国会で可決され、自衛隊をカンボジアでの平和維持活動に合法的に派遣させることが可能になりました。これに続き、1992年にアンゴラ、1993～95年にモザンビーク、1994年にエルサルバドルへ、それぞれ選挙監視協力を行うため自衛隊が派遣されました。自衛隊は1996年、ゴラン高原でのイスラエルとシリアの停戦監視部隊としても活動しました。1999年には東ティモールのPKO活動にも自衛隊員113名が参加しました。

国連のPKOへの協力により、日本は国際紛争の解決にカネを出すだけという海外の批判を和らげるための、重要な意思表示を行いました。日本の自衛隊がカンボジアと東ティモール活動で立派な成績をあげたことから、2001年の9・11後のイラク戦争への派遣は国際的

Many Americans felt that the Japanese were selfish in depending on the U.S. military to defend Japan's supply of petroleum. Japan imports over half of its petroleum from the Gulf States, their reasoning went, and Japan should send troops to participate in the fighting, placing Japanese lives alongside American lives. In the background is the fact that Japanese taxpayers were paying far less for defense than Americans. The Japanese government imposed a ceiling of 1% of the GNP on defense expenditures. In 1992 for example, that meant $275 per capita. In the same year, the U.S. devoted 5% of its GNP, amounting to $1,122 per capita. Rather naturally, from the American point of view, Japan should have been increasing its share of the costs.

Only after intense domestic debate did the Diet in 1992 pass the Law on Cooperation in United Nations Peacekeeping Operations, enabling the government to legally dispatch Self-Defense Forces to participate in peacekeeping operations in Cambodia. This was followed by SDF assistance in supervising elections in Angola in 1992, Mozambique in 1993–1995 and El Salvador in 1994. The SDF also served as observers of the truce on the **Golan Heights** between Israel and Syria in 1996. In 1999 113 SDF members joined a UN Peacekeeping Operation in East Timor.

As a result of joining UN PKO operations, Japan made a significant **gesture** toward appeasing criticism from abroad that Japan only made financial contributions to solving international disputes. Because Japan's SDF had a good record in its activities in Cambodia and

により広く受け入れられました。それに対して、多くの日本人は、国連の活動への協力にも依然として不安を抱いていました。その理由の一端として、保守派が、PKO協力が日本における軍隊の役割を「**正常化**」する契機と考えていたことがありました。

日本周辺国の軍備状況
Military Capabilities in Region Surrounding Japan

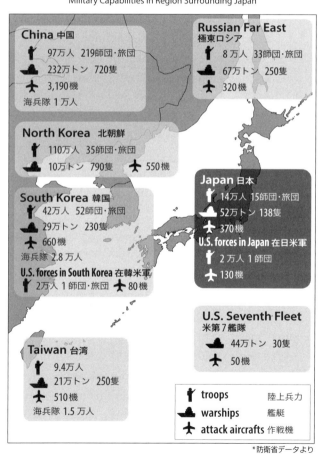

China 中国
97万人　219師団・旅団
232万トン　720隻
3,190機
海兵隊 1万人

Russian Far East
極東ロシア
8万人　33師団・旅団
67万トン　250隻
320機

North Korea 北朝鮮
110万人　35師団・旅団
10万トン　790隻　550機

Japan 日本
14万人　15師団・旅団
52万トン　138隻
370機
U.S. forces in Japan 在日米軍
2万人　1師団
130機

South Korea 韓国
42万人　52師団・旅団
29万トン　230隻
660機
海兵隊 2.8万人
U.S. forces in South Korea 在韓米軍
2万人　1師団・旅団　80機

U.S. Seventh Fleet
米第7艦隊
44万トン　30隻
50機

Taiwan 台湾
9.4万人
21万トン　250隻
510機
海兵隊 1.5万人

troops　　　　　　陸上兵力
warships　　　　　艦艇
attack aircrafts　作戦機

*防衛省データより

East Timor, there was greater international acceptance of its deployment in the Iraq war after September 11, 2001. Many Japanese, to the contrary, remained uneasy about participation even in UN operations, partly because conservatives at home were seeing PKO partic-ipation as the beginning of "**normalization**" of the role of the military in Japan.

㉛ 「不戦決議」と「村山談話」

1994年6月、自由民主党・日本社会党・新党さきがけの3党からなる「自社さ連立政権」が発足し、村山富市（社会党）内閣がスタートしました。

村山内閣の1995年、衆議院に「歴史を教訓に平和への決意を新たにする決議（不戦決議）」が提出されました。社会党が草案を提出、自民党の反発により大幅な修正がなされましたが、衆議院502議員中251人が投票、230人が支持票を投じました。その決議では、「全世界の戦没者、戦争の犠牲者に哀悼の誠を捧げ、植民地支配や侵略的行為について深い反省の念を表明し、日本国憲法の掲げる恒久平和の理念の下、人類共生の未来を切り開く決意」の表明がなされました。

また、1995年の8月15日の戦後50周年記念式典において、村山首相は、閣議決定に基づき、戦中・戦前に日本が行った「侵略」や「植民地支配」について、政府として正式に謝罪しました。これは「村山談話」と呼ばれ、現在も政府の公式見解となっています。この後、村山首相は、アジア各国を歴訪し日本の過去の「侵略戦争」のお詫びをする「謝罪外交」を展開しました。

90年代経済問題の教訓

　日本国内では、過去40年間に想像もしなかったような試練に直面しました。まず、1980年代後半のバブル経済が崩壊し、回復の糸口がまったく見つからない長期的な景気後退となりました。

　経済問題は、特にドルが高かった1980年代初頭の米国による日本の輸入品消費が一因でした。1985年には為替レートは1ドル＝260円まで上がりました。米国の労働者は、国内生産製品よりも輸入品を購入していました。言うまでもなく、その結果として、雇用は落ち込み、「リストラ」が続きました。もう一つの衝撃は、より多くの工場が海外に移転したことでした。その結果、予想されたように、**慢性的な貿易不均衡**を生み、米国の保護主義者は再び輸入品への規制を要請しました。

　「リストラ」は米国に限ったことではありませんでした。日本にも同様に強い影響を及ぼしました。「リストラ」は、日本で、45～54歳に最も厳しいものでした。労働力の高齢化により、高所得・低生産の従業員の比率が上昇し、企業の負担となりました。彼らは大概、最も人件費がかかり、新たな技術に最も疎く、**能力給制度**に最も適応できない人々でした。経費削減の時代に、この年齢層はリストラの主な標的となったのです。1990年代後半まで、

Economic Lessons of the 1990s

At home, Japan faced challenges that would not have been imagined in the previous four decades. First was the bursting of the economic bubble of the late 1980s which was followed by a prolonged recession which no one seemed to have a remedy for.

Part of the economic problems was brought on by America's consumption of imports from Japan during the early 1980s when the dollar was particularly strong. In 1985, the exchange rate went as high as ¥260 to the dollar. Rather than buying products produced in the U.S. by U.S. workers, Americans were purchasing imports. One result, of course, was a decline in employment rates as "restructuring" continued. A second impact was that more factories were moved overseas. As could be expected, the result was a **chronic trade imbalance**, and American protectionists began to call once again for restrictions on imports.

"Restructuring" was not limited to America. It had a major impact on Japan as well. In Japan "restructuring" hit hardest the age group between 45 and 54. The aging workforce has saddled firms with a rising proportion of well-paid but less-productive senior employees. They are usually the most expensive employees, the least adept at newer technologies and the least able to adapt to **merit-based wage scales**. In an age of cost-cutting, this age group has become the central target of restructuring. By the late 1990s, the media carried stories of how firms

メディアは、企業が、**年金**や**退職金**を減らし、窓際のポストや子会社に左遷させたりして男性幹部社員を退職に追い込んでいる状況を伝えました。何十年と会社に忠誠を尽くしてきた年配の従業員にとって、そのような扱いは彼らの信頼と忍耐を完全に裏切るものになりました。ひとたび仕事を失えば、彼らがそれまで得てきた収入に近い給料を得られる職を新たに見つけるのは極めて困難でした。

円・ドル相場が貿易収支に及ぼす影響に話を戻しましょう。1985年9月、世界の主要工業国の代表がニューヨークのプラザホテルに集まり、各国の保護貿易主義の高まりを是正し、自由貿易システムを守るために議論しました。いわゆる**プラザ合意**は、基本的にはドル安、円高を進めることで合意されました。そこで意図されていたのは、米国市場の外国製品の価格を引き上げて貿易収支を是正することでした。このようにして外国製品の魅力を下げ、貿易相手国に米国製品の購入を促そうとしたのです。

円相場は一気に倍に跳ね上がり、10年後には驚異的な1ドル＝83円になりました。日本政府は税を引き下げ、貸付金利を減らし、信用条件を緩和させることで、国内消費を高めようとしました。

しかし、プラザ合意では状況は改善されませんでした。円高により、日本のメーカーは原料をより低い価格で輸入でき、生産費を抑えることができたのです。そして、日本の輸出品

were pushing senior male employees into retirement by reducing **pension** and **severance payments,** by assigning them to menial jobs and even assigning them to subsidiary companies. To older employees who had loyally served their companies for decades, such treatment amounted to total betrayal of their trust and perseverance. Once they had lost their jobs, it was extremely difficult to find a new job that paid anywhere near what they had been earning until then.

Let us return to the issue of the impact of the yen-dollar rate on the balance of trade. Leaders of the world's industrial powers gathered at the Plaza Hotel in New York in September 1985 to work out a way to prevent the raising of protectionist barriers in each country and to protect the system of free trade. The so-called **Plaza Accord** that they agreed to consisted in strengthening the yen and weakening the dollar. The intended goal was to correct the balance of trade by increasing the prices of foreign goods in American markets. This would supposedly make foreign goods less attractive and encourage trading partners to buy more U.S. goods.

The value of the yen quickly doubled—and ten years later it would reach an astounding $1 = ¥83. The Japanese government attempted to boost domestic consumption by lowering taxes, reducing interest rates for loans and making credit easier to obtain.

But the Plaza Accord did not improve the situation. The stronger yen allowed Japanese manufacturers to import materials at lower prices, and this lowered costs of production. This in turn further increased the appeal

の魅力がさらに高まり、日本企業の景気は良くなりました。「高度成長」に戻ったようでした。

1986年になると、日本の海外投資に関する報道が日常化しました。日本の不動産会社はハワイやカリフォルニアの有名ホテル、ゴルフ場を買収しました。ソニーはコロンビア映画を買収しました。松下電器がMCAを買収した際は、MCAが米国で最も人気の高いリゾート地の一つ、ヨセミテ国立公園の施設を所有していたため、米国の国民感情を刺激しました。米国紙は、「日本株式会社」の米国乗っ取りに関する記事を掲載しました。その間、日本国内では地価と不動産価格が高騰し、1986年1月から1989年12月までの間に**日経平均株価指数**は約3倍の3万9000円台近くに跳ね上がりました。

しかし、過熱した経済は持続できず、いわゆる「バブル経済」は最終的にはじけました。収益の低下、**新興工業国**との新たな競合、欧米先進諸国の景気後退などによって、収益を維持できなくなったのです。1989年12月から1年で、株価は40%も下落しました。株価は2003年8月30日には7604円まで落ち込みました。経済的苦境をさらに悪化させたこととして、長く議論されていた3%の消費税――ヨーロッパ諸国と比べると低い――が1989年初頭に導入されました。

企業は経費を削減し、従業員は「リストラ」され、新卒は就職口を見つけられず、定期預金利率は0.1%を切り、一般家庭の収入は横ばい状態でした。映画産業では、松下電器がMCA

of Japanese exports and left Japanese corporations flush with cash. "High-growth" seemed to have returned.

Beginning in 1986, Japanese investment overseas made regular headlines. Japanese real estate firms bought famous hotels and golf courses in Hawaii and California. Sony Corporation bought Columbia Pictures. Matsushita bought MCA, which aroused the American public because MCA owned facilities in Yosemite National Park, America's number one most popular natural vacation site. American newspapers carried articles about the takeover of America by "Japan, Inc." Meanwhile back in Japan, housing and land prices spiraled upwards and between January 1986 and December 1989 the **Nikkei stock index** tripled to nearly ¥39,000.

But the overheated economy was unsustainable and the so-called "bubble economy" finally burst. With declining profits, competition from **newly developing economies** and recession in the Western industrialized nations, it was impossible to keep the profits coming in. Within twelve months of December 1989, the Nikkei plunged 40%. It ultimately reached a bottom of ¥7,604 on August 30, 2003. To compound the economic difficulties, the long-debated consumption tax of 3%—small by comparison with European nations—went into effect in early 1989. That tax was raised in 1997 to 5%.

Companies retrenched, employees were "restructured," new graduates could not find jobs, savings accounts earned less than a tenth of a percent and household incomes remained flat. On the big screen, Matsushita

の叩き売りを余儀なくされ、ソニーはコロンビア映画をなんとか維持する状況でした。

長い目で見れば、経済の足を引っ張ったのは**不良債権**でした。慎重さに欠けた投資家が、株や不動産を取得するために巨額の融資を受け、返済できなくなりました。大企業だけでなく個人も「財テク」で利益を得ようとしました。すべての企業のすべての社員が金儲けしているかに見えた時期、彼らは過度の危険を冒したのです。その結果、銀行が実質的にすべての人への貸付を拒むという大規模な貸し渋りが起こりました。

1998年までに大手証券2社、三洋証券と山一證券、さらに、北海道拓殖銀行が破綻しました。元来低かった日本の失業率は記録を更新しました。**経営破綻**の件数は、戦後最高を記録しました。国内総生産（GDP）は減少を続けました。日本は新しい世紀を目の前にして、栄光の日々は過ぎ去ったと考えられました。

自民党の衰退

1990年代における第2の国内問題は、自民党の派閥と地元利益優先政治の破綻でした。

竹下登首相は1989年春、リクルートコスモ

was forced to sell MCA at a deep discount and Sony barely managed to hold onto Columbia Pictures.

Dragging the economy down in the long run were **nonperforming loans**. Investors who lacked caution had borrowed huge sums to finance acquisitions of stock and real estate, and now they were unable to repay the loans. Individuals as well as major corporations had attempted to profit through what came to be called *zai-teku*, financial management technique. They had taken on excessive risk when it seemed that everyone was making money at every enterprise. The result was a major credit crunch as banks refused to lend money to virtually everyone.

By 1998 two of Japan's leading brokerage firms, Sanyo and Yamaichi Securities, and the Hokkaido Takushoku Bank went under. Japan's traditionally low unemployment rate reached a new high. **Business bankruptcies** reached a high for the postwar period. The GDP continued to decline. As Japan awaited the turn of the millennium, there were serious reasons to believe that its best days were in the past.

LDP Decline

The second domestic challenge of the 1990s was the breakdown of the LDP factions and local-interest based politics.

Prime Minister Takeshita Noboru was forced to

ス社から**不正献金**を受けていたことが発覚し、辞任に追い込まれました。竹下に続き、宇野宗佑首相も、長く愛人関係にあった芸者に口止め料を払ったことが明るみになり、わずか2カ月で退陣しました。1993年には自民党副総裁の金丸信が、佐川急便から不正献金を受領していたことから逮捕されました。一般市民は、警察の捜査で金丸の事務所、自宅から10億円相当の金塊が見つかったと聞いて、大いに盛り上がりました。

　その後に続いたのは、自民党所属の数人の**凡庸な**首相たちで、一度政府の指導者になれば目標は達したと言わんばかりでした。二大政党政治によるより多元的システムが登場するかについての臆測がなされました。

　1996年に創設された民主党の菅直人と鳩山由紀夫は、政官業の癒着の徹底的な打破を打ち出しました。それは、例えば、早期退職した官僚がかつて監督していた企業の有閑職に再就職する天下り、文字通り天国からの光臨の構造に終止符を打つことによってでした。この構造がいかに癒着に結びつきやすいかは、2005年に横河ブリッジ社が橋を建設する公共事業の**談合入札**に関与したことから明らかになりました。

　民主党は2004年総選挙で与党自民党の最大のライバルになりましたが、人気があった菅直人が年金スキャンダルから党代表を辞任

resign in the spring of 1989 over the discovery that he had accepted **illegal donations** from Recruit Cosmos. Following Takeshita was Prime Minister Uno Sosuke who lasted a mere two months in office after it became known that he had paid hush money to a geisha not to tell about their long-term affair. In 1993 Deputy Prime Minister Kanemaru Shin was arrested for accepting illegal contributions from parcel delivery service Sagawa Kyubin. The public was greatly entertained to learn that police raids on Kanemaru's office and home had uncovered a billion yen's worth of gold bars.

What followed were several **uninspiring**, short-term LDP prime ministers who seemed to have no other goals than to serve once as the leader of the government. Speculation arose about whether a more pluralistic system of two-party politics might emerge.

Kan Naoto and Hatoyama Yukio of the Democratic Party of Japan (DPJ) (*Minshuto*), founded in 1996, began arguing for a decisive break in the collusive ties between bureaucrats, politicians and business, for example, by ending the *amakudari* system, literally "descent from heaven," which landed early retiring bureaucrats in cushy posts in businesses which they had earlier supervised. An example of how open this system was to collusion came to light in 2005 when Yokogawa Bridge Corporation was involved in **rigging bids** for public bridge construction projects.

The DPJ became the primary rival of the ruling LDP in the elections of 2004, but when the popular Kan Naoto became involved in a pension scandal and

せざるをえなくなり、民主党の支持は下落しました。2003年に衆議院で実質的に178議席を確保していた民主党は、2005年の総選挙で62議席を失い、日本には米国の共和党と民主党のような二大政党制の準備が整っているのか、疑問も投げかけられました。

戦後日本の歴代首相

歴代	首相名	就任年	所属政党	在職日数（累計）
第42代	鈴木 貫太郎	1945	——	133日
第43代	東久邇宮 稔彦王	1945	同和会	54日
第44代	幣原 喜重郎	1945	貴族院	226日
第45代	吉田 茂①	1946	日本自由党	368日
第46代	片山 哲	1947	日本社会党	296日
第47代	芦田 均	1948	民主党	220日
第48〜51代	吉田 茂②〜⑤	1948	民主自由党、自由党	2248日
第52〜54代	鳩山 一郎①〜③	1954	日本民主党、自由民主党	745日
第55代	石橋 湛山	1956	自由民主党	65日
第56〜57代	岸 信介①〜②	1957	自由民主党	1241日
第58〜60代	池田 勇人①〜③	1960	自由民主党	1575日
第61〜63代	佐藤 栄作①〜③	1964	自由民主党	2798日
第64〜65代	田中 角栄①〜②	1972	自由民主党	886日
第66代	三木 武夫	1974	自由民主党	747日
第67代	福田 赳夫	1976	自由民主党	714日
第68〜69代	大平 正芳①〜②	1978	自由民主党	554日
第70代	鈴木 善幸	1980	自由民主党	864日
第71〜73代	中曽根 康弘①〜③	1982	自由民主党	1806日
第74代	竹下 登	1987	自由民主党	576日

had to resign as party president, support of the party slid. From a substantial 178 seats in the House of Representatives in 2003, the DPJ lost 62 members in the 2005 parliamentary elections, casting doubts on Japan's readiness for a two-party system like the Republicans and Democrats of the U.S.

Postwar Japanese Prime Ministers

歴代	首相名	就任年	所属政党	在職日数（累計）
第75代	宇野 宗佑	1989	自由民主党	69日
第76～77代	海部 俊樹 ①～②	1989	自由民主党	818日
第78代	宮澤 喜一	1991	自由民主党	644日
第79代	細川 護煕	1993	日本新党	263日
第80代	羽田 孜	1994	新生党	64日
第81代	村山 富市	1994	日本社会党	561日
第82～83代	橋本 龍太郎 ①～②	1996	自由民主党	932日
第84代	小渕 恵三	1998	自由民主党	616日
第85～86代	森 喜朗 ①～②	2000	自由民主党	387日
第87～89代	小泉 純一郎 ①～③	2001	自由民主党	1980日
第90代	安倍 晋三 ①	2006	自由民主党	366日
第91代	福田 康夫	2007	自由民主党	365日
第92代	麻生 太郎	2008	自由民主党	358日
第93代	鳩山 由紀夫	2009	民主党	266日
第94代	菅 直人	2010	民主党	452日
第95代	野田 佳彦	2011	民主党	482日
第96～98代	安倍 晋三 ②～④	2012	自由民主党	3188日
第99代	菅 義偉	2020	自由民主党	384日
第100～101代	岸田 文雄 ①～②	2021	自由民主党	

改革への道

　巨大な公社の基本的改革は、日本国有鉄道と日本電信電話公社の**民営化**から始まりました。これらの事業体を「民営化」するというのは、実際には、これらを「売却」し、新企業に売却で出た巨額の資金を運用させて、政府の補助金を受けずに運営させることを意味しました。総じて、サービスも著しく向上しました。

　1990年代後半、政府は金融制度の**規制を緩和する**総合計画を実施しました。1997年から2001年にかけて順次実現した「ビッグバン」は、銀行、保険、証券業界の非効率性をもたらしていた規制を緩和することが狙いでした。金融制度改革の中心、公的資金を利用することで、**債務超過の銀行**を買収し、**不良債権を整理**することでした。「バブル経済」の間、銀行は、生産を伸ばしたい企業や巨大事業投資家に融資しました。誰もが容易に金儲けをしていたような時代、銀行は、リスクは最小と決め込み、融資する前に慎重にリスクを評価することはほとんどありませんでした。銀行はさらに、株や不動産の投機家にも融資するという過ちを犯しました。バブルがはじけると**担保物件**の価値は減少し、銀行は貸付金の回収ができなくなったのです。

　銀行は何年も不良債権処理に積極的に取り組まなかったようで、結局、金融制度全体が不

Road to Reform

Essential reforms of the huge public corporations began with the **privatization** of Japan National Railway (JNR) and the Public Telephone Company. "Privatizing" these entities essentially meant "selling" them and this saved huge sums of money by forcing the new corporations to operate without government subsidies. By most accounts, the service also improved considerably.

In the late 1990s the government implemented a comprehensive program to **deregulate** the financial system. The so-called "big bang," which actually occurred gradually from 1997 through 2001, sought to ease regulations that caused the banking, insurance and securities industries to operate inefficiency. A major part of the reform of the banking system was the use of public funds to take over **insolvent banks** and **liquidate their bad debt**. During the "bubble economy" the banks had offered loans to companies to expand production capacity and to speculators in mega-projects. Since it seemed that everyone was making money easily, the banks assumed that risks were minimal and they rarely assessed the risks carefully before lending the money. They made a further mistake in lending money to speculators in stocks and real estate. When the bubble burst, the value of the **collateral** shrank and the banks were unable to get their money back.

For years the banks seemed unwilling to write off the bad loans, leaving the entire banking system unstable.

安定になりました。政治家は当初、解決策を推進することを渋りましたが、結局は国の経済を回復させる必要性が大規模な改革を促しました。

小泉純一郎が2001年に首相に就任すると、経済政策のさらなる劇的変革を掲げ、銀行の不良債権への強硬対応、郵政民営化、政策決定の**地方分権化**を打ち出しました。

中央政府から自治体へ

日本は長い間、極めて**中央集権的な**国家と見なされてきました。しかし2004年、小泉首相は、自治体に対し、中央政府の補助金の大幅な削減に対処すべく提言をまとめるよう求める、大胆な措置を取りました。このような権限移譲は、地方の政策決定主体への**税源移譲**を伴いました。

このような権限委譲は、それまで中央政府が地方自治体に対して維持していたコントロールの程度を変えるものとされました。自治体により大きな自治権を与えることで、二つの好影響が期待されました。第1は、中央政府の支出削減です。第2は、自治体が税収の用途を自由に決定できるようになることです。しかし、こうした移譲は、中央政府の支援を失っ

Politicians were initially unwilling to force a resolution, but finally the need to rejuvenate the nation's economy prompted major reform.

When Koizumi Jun'ichiro assumed the post of prime minister in 2001, he pledged another round of dramatic changes in economic policies, including a hard line on non-performing bank loans, privatization of postal services and the **decentralization** of government decision-making.

From Central Government to Local Government

Japan has long been seen as a strongly **centralized** nation, but in 2004 Prime Minister Koizumi took the bold step of urging local governments to put together proposals for dealing with a major reduction in subsidies from the central government. Such a transfer of power would be accompanied by a **transfer of tax revenue** to the local decision-making bodies.

Such a transfer would change the degree of control which the central government had until then maintained over the local governments. Giving the local governments more autonomy would have two positive impacts. First, it would reduce the expenditures of the central government. Second, it would allow the local governments freedom to decide how tax revenues ought to be spent. The negative impact is that such a transfer would

た自治体に、サービスを負担させるという否定的影響もあります。

　地方分権政策、いわゆる「三位一体改革」は、2006年現在、ほとんど成果をあげていませんが、日本が公的部門の改革を成し遂げようとするなら、根本的な問題を何とか解決しなければならないでしょう。

情報社会の試練

　1990年代後半、インターネットは日本で不可欠な手段となり、より多くの人がショッピング、通信、リサーチ、情報収集、銀行業務、カタログ注文、証券取引など日々の活動をインターネットで行うようになりました。インターネットアクセス機能を持つ世帯の比率は、1996年に約3%だったのが21世紀になると19%に上がり、2003年には88%に急上昇しました。インターネットを利用する個人の比率は、2002年初めの35%から2005年末の47%に増加しました。

　今や「インターネット・バブル」と——「ドットコム・バブル」「ITバブル」とも——言われるなか、インターネット関連のベンチャー企業は世界中で急成長しました。投資家は、巨額の利益を期待できそうな企業に熱心に資金を注ぎました。その結果、米国のナスダック株式市場の平均株価は、1996年の1000ドル水準か

place the burden for providing services on the local government without support from the central government.

The decentralization policy, so-called "trinity reform *sanmi ittai*", met with no success as of 2006, but the underlying problems will have to be resolved in some way if Japan is to achieve public sector restructuring.

Trials of the Information Society

During the latter half of the 1990s, the Internet became an essential tool in Japan, with more people going online to conduct day-to-day activities such as shopping, correspondence, research and information-gathering, banking, catalogue-ordering and even stock-trading. The percentage of households with Internet access began at approximately 3% in 1996, rose to 19% by the turn of the century and then streaked to 88% in 2003. Individual use of the Internet rose from 35% in early 2002 to 47% in late 2005.

In what is now referred to as the "Internet Bubble" —also called the "dot-com bubble" or "IT bubble"— Internet-related venture companies around the world showed extremely rapid growth. Investors were eagerly pouring money into companies which seemed to promise enormous profits. As a result, average prices on America's NASDAQ exchange saw an increase from $1,000 levels in 1996 to $5,000 levels in 2000. When

ら2000年には5000ドル水準に値上がりしました。投資家が「ニュー・エコノミー」に対して、より現実的な態度を取るようになると、新興企業の市場が暴落し、2002年までに平均株価は約1000ドル水準に逆戻りしました。

生き残った海外のベンチャー企業としては、グーグル、アマゾン・ドット・コム、イーベイが最も良く知られています。日本のIT関連企業ではソフトバンク、楽天、ヤフーが生き残り、ほかは事業を縮小するかまたは完全に姿を消しました。

2005年、途方もない楽天家のマンガキャラクターにちなんで「ホリエモン」として知られた、ライブドア代表の堀江貴文が頻繁にメディアに登場しました。「カネがあればなんでもできる」のセリフで有名になった当時33歳のCEOは、デザイナーズTシャツに身を包み、従来の日本のビジネスのやり方に一人で挑んでいるように見えました。彼は27の企業を買収し、収益は想像もつかないほどに膨れ上がりました。フジサンケイグループの**敵対的買収**——実現していれば日本で初めてとなった——にも乗り出しました。シックな六本木ヒルズに本社を構えた彼は、インターネット世代のヒーローでした。

ライブドアが入居する六本木ヒルズ森タワー
（2006年1月）

investors became more realistic about the so-called "new economy," the market for start-ups collapsed, and by 2002, the average shares on that exchange were back down to about $1,000.

Of the survivors abroad, Google, Amazon.com, and e-Bay are among the best-known. Of the IT-related firms in Japan, Softbank, Rakuten and Yahoo survived, while others shrank or disappeared entirely.

During 2005 Horie Takafumi, known widely as "Horiemon" after a boundlessly optimistic cartoon character, appeared regularly in the news representing Livedoor Co. Famous for saying, "you can do anything with money," the then 33-year-old designer-T-shirt-wearing CEO seemed to single-handedly challenge the way business was done in Japan. He had acquired 27 companies and increased revenues beyond imagination's grasp. He even launched a **hostile takeover**—which would have been the first in Japan—of the broadcasting group Fujisankei Communications. Established in his chic Roppongi Hills headquarters, he was a hero for the Internet age.

Late in 2005, however, the "Horiemon phenomenon" began to unravel. Investigators began looking into allegations of irregularities in how Livedoor did business. As a result, in January 2006, Horie was arrested and a new team of executives took over Livedoor. Tokyo District Public Prosecutors in February indicted Horie and three former executives of the Livedoor group on charges of violating the Securities and Exchange Law. They were accused of spreading false information to

しかし、2005年末、「ホリエモン現象」の実態が露呈し始めました。ライブドアの経営方法における不正行為に調査が入りました。結局、2006年1月に堀江は逮捕され、ライブドアには新しい経営幹部が就任しました。東京地方検察庁は2月に堀江とライブドアの元役員3人を証券取引法違反で起訴しました。彼らは、株価をつり上げるために虚偽の情報を流布し、ライブドアの**粉飾決算**を行っていたとして告発されました。確かに、彼らは株式分割、M&A（合併・買収）、投資会社など新しい手法を用いましたが、情報のでっち上げとは古いやり方でした。

　日本国内でライブドアの汚職は、国が向かう方向性についての論争を引き起こしました。日本経済はバブル崩壊後15年続いた景気後退からようやく健全な状態に戻ったところでした。企業は再び経常黒字を記録し、賃金は上昇し、雇用も増えていました。13年ぶりに求職者数と雇用数が一致した矢先に汚職が発覚したのです。汚職が起きたことで一般の人々は、ライブドアが、不適切な金融・株式規制、あまりにも急速な市場の自由化、合併・買収の危険性といった様々な問題の見本だったのか、と思いを巡らしました。

jack up share prices and **cooking** Livedoor's **account books**. True enough, they used new methods including share splitting, mergers and acquisitions and investment funds, but the fabrication of information was an old trick.

Within Japan, the Livedoor scandal stirred controversy over the direction in which the country was headed. Japan's economy was just returning to health after a 15-year post-bubble slump. Companies were making record profits again, wages were on the rise and jobs were on the increase. As the scandal broke, for the first time in 13 years there was a job for everyone who wanted one. With the scandal, the public wondered whether Livedoor was somehow representative of broader problems—of inadequate financial and stock-market regulations, excessively rapid liberalization of markets, and the dangers of mergers and acquisitions.

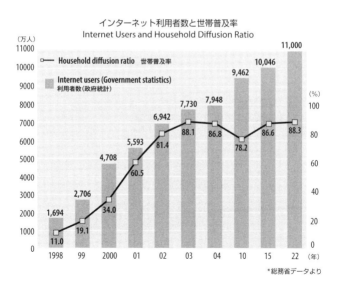

インターネット利用者数と世帯普及率
Internet Users and Household Diffusion Ratio

*総務省データより

1月18日、堀江のオフィス、自宅に強制捜査が入った翌日、**東京証券取引所**には、ライブドア銘柄だけでなく、ほかのインターネット関連銘柄も、売り注文が殺到しました。数日のうちにインターネット企業以外の銘柄も下落し始めました。株価急落は、東京証券取引所そのものの脆弱性も露呈しました。強制捜査の翌日、取引所が対応できる件数を約定数が超えそうになり、取引が史上初めて早期停止となりました。その後数週間、「不測の事態」として、ライブドア株の取引を午後2時から午後3時までに限定しました。

　ライブドア問題を受けて、監視体制やコーポレート・ガバナンス、情報開示の改善がなされるかどうかはまだ分かりません。ただし、情報技術とインターネットを不可欠な手段としてフル活用しない企業には利益がもたらされないことは確かなようです

輸出される日本文化

　日本のアニメは国内だけでなく海外でも成功を収めました。世界中でテレビ放映されているアニメ漫画番組の約60%が、日本で製作されたものです。例えば『ポケモン』のテレビシリーズは60カ国以上で放送されています。日本のアニメ映画の人気で、アニメーション

On January 18, the day after investigators raided Horie's office and residence, the **Tokyo Stock Exchange** (TSE) was flooded with orders to sell not only Livedoor shares but other Internet-related shares as well. Within a few days, shares of even non-Internet companies were dropping in value. The sell-off exposed a weakness in the TSE itself. The number of transactions on the day after the raid came close to exceeding the number the exchange could handle and the exchange itself was shut down early, for the first time in its history. For weeks afterward the trading of Livedoor stock was limited to one hour from two to three in the afternoon, "an emergency measure."

It remained to be seen whether improvement in surveillance, corporate governance and disclosure would be made as a result of the Livedoor problems. But it seemed clear that there could be no return to business that did not make full use of Information Technology and the Internet as essential tools.

Cultural Exports

Japanese anime has become a huge success not only in Japan but also overseas. Some 60% of the animated cartoon programs shown on television around the world are produced in Japan. The "Pokémon" TV series, for example, has been shown in more than 60 countries. Japanese animated films have become so popular that

を略した「アニメ」という日本語が多くの外国語で使われるようになったほどです。

宮崎駿のアニメ映画『ハウルの動く城』を制作したスタジオジブリは、2004年9月にベネチア国際映画祭でオゼッラ技術貢献賞を受賞しました。著名な監督にとって3度目となる主要な国際賞の受賞でした。『千と千尋の神隠し』が、ベルリン国際映画祭金熊賞、第75回アカデミー賞長編アニメ映画賞を受賞しています。

日本の映画、テレビシリーズの収益は、キャラクターグッズの収益を含め、2004年には米国だけで43億ドルに達し、いかに海外で飛躍しているかが分かります。これは、日本の鉄鋼製品の米国市場での収益の3倍、米国への日本の総輸出の3.5%を占めています。

アニメが日本の有力なコンテンツ・ビジネ

🐢 海外に紹介された日本文化

　欧米が日本近代小説の英訳に関心を持つようになったのは、第2次世界大戦後のことでした。1955年に大佛次郎の『帰郷』と谷崎潤一郎の『蓼喰う虫』の翻訳版が登場し、西洋が敵対国だった日本を理解し始めるきっかけを作りました。しかしどちらの作品も意図されたところは、かつての日本の探求でした。重要なのは、ある種風変わりな土地として日本を描き、それが特に米国人読者には魅力的だったことです。ある意味でどちらの小説も、日本が許しがたい敵から冷戦期の不可欠な同盟国へと変貌するときに「適切なイメージ」を与えたのです。『帰郷』は「まったく新しい、新鮮な日本の光景」を紹介していると評されました。実際のところ両作品ともにラフカディオ・ハーンや岡倉天心によって有名になった

"*anime*," the shortened Japanese word for "animation," has become a new word in many other languages.

In September 2004, Studio Ghibli, which produced Miyazaki Hayao's animated film "Howl's Moving Castle," received the Osella outstanding technical contribution award at the Venice Film Festival. It was the third major international award for the famed director. "Spirited Away" won the first animated film to win the Golden Bear prize at the Berlin International Film Festival and Best Animated Feature Film at the 75th Academy Awards.

Illustrating how significant Japanese movies and TV series are abroad, in the U.S. alone, together with character goods, they earned $4.3 billion in 2004. That is three times the size of the U.S. market for Japanese steel products and 3.5% of the total exports from Japan to the U.S.

While *anime* is one of the leading content

戦前の日本のイメージにより近いものでした。戦時中の日本は好戦的な男社会と捉えられていたが、翻訳された小説を通じてより穏やかで女性的な社会の日本が表現された、という評価もありました。

1950年代、米国の出版社は、3人の作家の名声を築きました。前出の谷崎、川端康成、三島由紀夫です。3人の作品の多くが翻訳、出版されたことは、日本文学の概念を米国人読者の心に定着させました。数十年間、新しい日本の作家はすべて、──米国人読者の見地からは──これら3人の作家が与えたイメージに一致するかどうかで判断されました。村上春樹と吉本ばななが名声を得て初めて、そのイメージは変わりました。

スの一つである一方、近年マンガも海外市場で劇的な成長を遂げています。マンガは西洋式に印刷するために絵柄を写真のように反転し、右とじ製本をしなければならず、何年も欧米諸国での販売は「失敗」に終わっていました。しかし2002年に、右から左に読む日本とまったく同じスタイルで全ページ製作された、まったく本物のマンガが初めて英語版で登場しました。それ以降、ある出版社は、ジャパニーズスタイルのマンガを描くための英語の「ハウツー」本まで出版しました。

皇位継承問題

天皇陛下の次男、秋篠宮文仁親王が1965年に生まれて以降、皇室では長く男子の**継承者**が生まれませんでした。秋篠宮文仁親王の妻、紀子妃が2006年9月6日に長男を**出産した**とき、全国にニュースがかけめぐり、人々は皇室の新しい家族の誕生を祝いました。宮内庁や政治家は別の理由で喜びました。というより、むしろ**ほっとした**のです。男子が誕生し、秋篠宮悠仁と名付けられたことは、皇位の男子による継承の維持を脅かす「皇位継承の危機」の解決を意味したからです。

「皇位継承の危機」が人々の間での、そして政治の領域で問題になったのは、皇太子徳仁

businesses of Japan, *manga* (graphic novels) have recently shown dramatic growth in the world market. For years, manga had to be "flopped" for sale in Western countries, with the images photographically reversed in order to be printed in the Western format, bound on the right-hand side. But in 2002, a totally authentic manga first appeared in English, with all of the pages in the original Japanese order, to be read right to left. Since then, one publisher has even published a "how to" book on drawing Japanese-style manga in English.

The Succession Controversy of the Imperial Throne

Since the birth of Prince Akishino, the current Emperor Akihito's second son, in 1965, there had been no male **heir** born in the family. When Princess Kiko, the wife of Prince Akishino, **gave birth to** her first son on September 6, 2006, the news flashed around the country and people celebrated the birth of a new member of the **Imperial household**. The Imperial Household Agency (IHA) and politicians had another reason to **rejoice**, or rather, **be relieved**: The birth of the boy, named Prince Hisahito of Akishino, was a solution to the "heir crisis" that threatened the continuity of male succession of the Chrysanthemum Throne.

The "heir crisis" became a public and political issue when it became likely that Princess Masako, married to

親王と結婚した雅子妃が将来の天皇を出産することがなさそうだと見こまれたころのことです。男子を出産しなければならないという**計り知れない重圧**を背負った雅子妃は、子をもうけましたが、2001年に生まれたその赤子は女子の愛子内親王でした。出産後まもなくして、雅子妃は**適応障害**となり、一般の人々の目に触れないようになって、皇室の一員としての公務から**身をひきました**。

このことは、**皇室典範**を改正して女性の子孫が皇位を継承することを認めるか否かについて、広範な議論をもたらしました。小泉純一郎首相（当時）は2005年、女子が皇位を継承することを認める皇室典範の改正案に対する支持を表明し、国民の支持を得ました。この改正案は、時代が変わり、女子が皇位につくことが許されるべきだと認めるものでした。

傍系皇族というかつて存在した家族構成を復活させることを唱える者もいました。この方法によれば、皇位継承者でなかった天皇の子は「傍系」の家族の長とされ、直系の皇族が男子の継承者をもうけられない場合には、皇位を継承する権利を持つものとされました。また、皇太子夫妻が、ほかの皇族から男子を**養子にとる**ことを認めようと提言する者もいました。多くの人が、皇室典範を改正して女子が天皇になることを認めるということに賛成し、前例——過去に計8人の皇后が皇位を継承しています——を持ち出して、その**慣行**に戻るべきときだと主張しました。しかし、**保守派の人々**

Crown Prince Naruhito, will not be giving birth to the future Emperor of Japan. Burdened by the **immense pressure** to bear a son, Princess Masako experienced difficulty in conceiving a child but in 2001 she gave birth to a baby girl, Princess Aiko. Soon after giving birth, Princess Masako **fell into depression** and **withdrew** from the public and her duties as a member of the Imperial household.

This led to a public debate on whether to amend the **law of the Imperial Household** to allow female descendants to succeed to the **throne**. In 2005, Prime Minister Koizumi Jun'ichiro announced his support of a bill to allow females to inherit the throne and won the support of the public, which recognized that times have changed and women should be allowed to **ascend the throne**.

Others suggested bringing back the historical structure of **collateral families**. Under this mechanism, an Emperor's son who was not a successor of the throne was made the head of a "collateral" family and had the right to ascend the throne if the main Imperial line was unable to produce a male heir. Others proposed allowing the Crown Prince and Princess to **adopt** a male child from another branch of the Imperial family. Many supported the new bill to allow women to take the throne, arguing that there was a precedent—a total of 8 empresses had succeeded to the throne—and it was time to bring back that **practice**. **Conservatives**, however, argued that since those empresses were not

は、皇后がその子に皇位を移譲することが認められていない以上、その地位は一時的なもので、男子の継承者が生まれるまでの**空白期間**を埋めるためのものだったにすぎないと主張しました。

悠仁親王の誕生により、皇位継承をめぐる議論は**下火**になりました。その赤子は、叔父の皇太子徳仁、父の秋篠宮文仁親王に次いで、皇位継承順位第3位となりました。皇室制度を変える緊急の必要性は低くなったように思われました。政府の動きが遅かった一方、批評家や専門家、さらには**宮内庁長官**までもが、状況が切迫していることと、確実な皇位継承を維持するために法制度を**改正**することの必要性を訴えました。この皇位継承の制度を変えることに対する賛否両論は、職場や社会、そして皇室内部で女性がいまなお直面している障害を浮き彫りにしました。日本人の多数が**両性の平等**を真に理解し、推進していくには、まだ長い時間がかかるように思われました。

リーマン・ショックと日本経済

多くの日本人にとって「リーマン」といえば「サラリーマン」のことを指します。このことばの省略形が同じ発音だからです。しかし、

allowed to pass on the right to the throne to their children, their status had only been temporary, to **fill in the gaps** in the male succession.

With the birth of Prince Hisahito, the succession controversy seemed to **subside**. The baby boy became the third in line of succession, following his uncle, the current Crown Prince Naruhito, and his father, Prince Akishino. It seemed that the urgency to change the system diminished. While the government was slow in taking action, critics, experts and even the **Grand Steward of the IHA** argued the urgency of the situation and the necessity to **amend** the law and system to maintain a steady succession. The various arguments for and against changing the system of succession seemed to highlight the barriers women still faced, whether at the workplace, in society or in the Imperial Household. It seemed it would be a long time before the majority of Japanese would truly understand and promote **gender equality**.

Lehman Shock and Japanese Economy

To many Japanese, the word "Lee-man" meant "salary men," as the shortened form had the same sound. After September 2008, however, the Japanese fast learned

2008年9月以降、日本人は、同じ名称の投資銀行が、世界を震撼させた**金融危機**の引き金の一つであることをすぐに知ることとなりました。

　当時、全米第4位の規模を誇った投資銀行リーマン・ブラザーズの**破綻**は、サブプライム・ローン問題やベア・スターンズの破綻など、米国経済に決定的な打撃を与えた一連の出来事のなかでも、最も衝撃的なものとなりました。リーマンの破綻は、日本経済にも**連鎖的な影響**をもたらすと考えられました。日本の銀行はサブプライム・ローンに深く関与しておらず、経済も米国と同じ速さで停滞していたわけではありませんでした。しかし、「米国がくしゃみをすれば、世界が風邪をひく」ということばの通り、米国における危機は世界中に急速に広がり、地球規模の金融危機をもたらしたのです。

　それでは、リーマンの破綻は日本にいかなる影響を与えたのでしょうか。破綻の直後、日本の銀行株は大きな打撃を受け、日経平均株価は3年ぶりの安値にまで下落しました。日本円は安全で安定した通貨と考えられたため、投資家はこぞって円買いに走り、円の価値を上げるに至りました。世界中の株式市場の下落は、日本商品の需要低下にもつながりました。このことは輸出の減少をもたらし、自動車メーカーなどの製造業を直撃し、さらにこれらのメーカーを支える自動車部品メーカーなどの中小企業に影響を及ぼしたのです。2008

of the investment bank with that name as one of the triggers of the major **financial crisis** that impacted the world.

In the United States, the **bankruptcy** of Lehman Brothers, the fourth-largest investment bank in the U.S. at that time, was the climax of a series of events that significantly damaged the economy, including the subprime loan crisis and the fall of other financial firms such as Bear Stearns. In Japan, the fall of Lehman seemed to have a **domino effect** on the economy. Japanese banks had not been deeply involved in subprime loans and the economy was not declining at the same rate as in the U.S. However, as the saying goes, "When America sneezes, the world catches a cold." The crisis in the U.S. spread rapidly throughout the world, leading to a global financial crisis.

So how did the Lehman collapse affect Japan? Immediately after the bankruptcy, Japanese bank stocks were hit hard, and the Nikkei Stock Average fell to its lowest level in 3 years. Since the Japanese yen was considered a safe and stable currency, investors rushed to buy yen, leading to a strengthened value of the yen. The sinking global stock markets also meant a decrease in demand for Japanese goods. This led to a cut in exports, directly hitting manufacturers in Japan, such as automobile manufacturers, which then affected the smaller companies that support those manufacturers, such as those specializing in car parts. The **steep**

年と2009年の**急速なGDPの減少**と経済状況は、1973年と1979年の「オイルショック」を思い起こさせます。

「リーマン・ショック」は雇用にも大きな影響を与えました。経済の**低迷**は経済活動の低下につながり、雇用の減少にもつながりました。業種に**関係なく**、企業は直接、間接に影響を受けました。多くはリストラと**雇用縮小**を余儀なくされ、なかでも非正規労働者に影響が及ぶ大規模な**解雇**を始めました。派遣切りとは、仲介業者から派遣される短期雇用者(派遣社員)や契約社員を「切る」という意味のことばであり、この時代を**特徴づける**ものとなりました。彼らは便利でコストもリスクも少ないため、日本の企業がこうした雇用形式に大きく依存している実態が明らかになりました。**停滞する経済**と減退する雇用の中で、解雇された労働者は新たな職を見つけることができず、日本はさらに深刻な不景気に陥りました。

「リーマン・ショック」は経済や社会に影響を及ぼしただけでなく、同時に恐ろしい構造的問題を**浮き彫り**にしました。国全体が本格的な不況となり、所得格差の拡大や賃金の減少に伴って、日本はより深刻な社会格差の拡大へと向かったのです。

decline of GDP in 2008 and 2009 and the economic situation were reminiscent of the "Oil Shocks" that occurred in 1973 and 1979.

The "Lehman Shock" had a major impact on employment as well. A **deteriorating** economy meant low levels of economic activities, which also meant less need for employees. Companies, **regardless of** industry, were affected both directly and indirectly. Many were required to restructure and **downsize their employment**, initiating major layoffs that particularly impacted the non-regular (full-time) workers. *Haken-giri*, a term for "cutting" the temporary employees (*haken*) or contract workers from agencies, was **characteristic** of this period. It brought to light how Japanese firms depended on these types of hiring, as they are convenient and require less cost and risk. With a **staggering economy** and declining employment, laid-off workers were unable to find new jobs, and Japan went into a deeper recession.

The "Lehman Shock" not only brought on economic and social consequences, but **highlighted** the grim structural problems as well. The entire country went into a major slump, and with the widening of the income gap and lowering of wages, Japan headed towards an even more severe widening of the social gap.

格差社会

長い間、日本人の多くは中流階級だと考えられてきました。それが現実か思い込みかはともかくとして、人々は実際、自らが中流階級に属していると考えていたのであり、1970年代には「一億総中流」という、日本は1億人の中流階級からなる国であるという意味のキャッチフレーズに、国民的なアイデンティティが見てとれました。

バブル崩壊後、1990年代半ばまでに、日本は景気後退によってもたらされたいわゆる「失われた10年」に入り、「フリーター」と呼ばれる企業に雇用されていない人々の増加をもたらしました。かつて**終身雇用**が約束された「サラリーマン」のモデルが崩壊し始めたのです。

2000年代初頭から、人々は自分が勝ち組、負け組のどちらに**属す**か考えるようになりました。それは単なる**人目を引く**レッテルではなく、現実の問題になったのです。日本は格差の拡大によって社会の分断が進行しており、格差社会といわれるようになりました。

格差は人々の生活の基本的なレベル、すなわち教育と雇用にまで達し、このことは生活のほかの領域にも影響を及ぼしました。私立の名門校、**学習塾**、一流大学といった良い教育——いずれも多額の費用がかかります——は職と**安定した**将来を守る上で役に立つと考

Disparate Society

It has been long thought that the majority of Japanese are middle class. Whether it was reality or **perception**, people actually saw themselves as belonging to the middle class, as represented in the national identity shared by the Japanese in the 1970s' catch phrase *ichi-oku so-churyu*, meaning that Japan was a country with a 100 million members of the middle class.

By the mid 1990s, after the bubble collapsed, Japan entered a so-called "lost decade" spurred by recession and leading to the growth of the unemployed, who were labeled as "freeters." What was once seen as the promised **life-time employment**-guaranteed "salaryman" model started to collapse.

In the early 2000s, people started categorizing themselves as **belonging to** either the *kachi-gumi*, the winner group, or the *make-gumi*, the loser group. It *was* not just a matter of **catchy** labels, but it became reality—Japan was becoming a divided society with a widening gap, calling itself *kakusa shakai*, a term combining the words "gap" or "disparity" and "society."

Disparity reached the fundamental levels of people's lives, that is, education and employment, which affect other parts of their lives. Good education, defined by private and prestigious schools, **cram schools**, and top universities—all of which come at a high price—would help secure employment and a **stable**

られていました。しかし、その機会は万人に与えられるのではなく、その余裕のある人だけに与えられるようになったのです。

不平等は雇用面でも広がりました。戦後、日本は終身雇用が保証された社会から、バブル崩壊に苦しむ経済、そしてより**階層化された**社会へと変容してきました。職場において、昇進は年齢より**成果**によって行われるようになりました。これは若年の就業者において最も顕著であり、彼らは**正社員**と非正規の従業員に分断されたようです。2001年から2006年にかけて、正社員の数は190万人減少し、非正規の従業員数は330万人増加しました。

家庭においても変化がみられました。かつては母親や妻は家庭で家事に勤しむ一方、父親や夫は一日中仕事をしていたものですが、いまでは**家計**を助けるために主婦がパートの仕事に就くことは普通になりました。生活費が高いことも一因ですが、さらに大きな理由としては、収入が減ったり、解雇されたり、正社員から非正規従業員になったりするという男性の雇用状況の変化がありました。多くの夫婦は子どもをもうける**余裕がない**と感じるようになりました。

厳しい経済状況をより具体的に示す**統計**もあります。厚生労働省は、2007年、日本のおよそ6人に1人が貧困状態にあると発表し、その15.7%という貧困率は、米国の17.1%に近

future. However, that opportunity was not available to everyone, only to those who could afford it.

Inequality also grew **in terms of** employment. During the postwar period, Japan went from being a society where people were guaranteed lifetime employment to an economy suffering from the bubble collapsing, then turning into a more **stratified** society. At the workplace, promotions came to be based less on seniority than on **performance**. That was most visible in the young generation of workers, who seem to be divided into the **full-time employee** and temporary worker groups. Between 2001 and 2006, the population of the regular-employed fell by 1.9 million, and the population of temporary workers rose by 3.3 million.

There were changes at home as well. Whereas mothers and wives formerly stayed at home to focus on housework while the fathers and husbands worked all day, it was now common for women to find part-time work to contribute to the **household income**. This was partly due to the high living expenses and, more significantly, the shift in employment status of the men, who earned less, suffered layoffs or worked full-time shifts as temporary workers. Many couples began to feel that they **could not afford to** have children.

Some **statistics** reveal the grim conditions more specifically. The Labor Ministry announced that almost 1 in 6 people in Japan lived in poverty in 2007, and the rate was close to that of the U.S., at 15.7% and

くなっています。経済協力開発機構（OECD）の報告によれば、1985年以降、日本における子どもの貧困率は14％に上昇しており、この数字はほかのOECD加盟国の平均を上回っています。

日本の人口は高齢化し、減少を続けています。雇用確保、安全、昇進の機会、退職後の生活の安心が減じてしまったのを目の当たりにして、国民は期待どころか希望さえ見出せなくなりつつあることは容易に理解できます。かつて日本人は「中流の国」神話に**固執**し、日本国内においては貧困を現実的な意味を持つ概念として認識していませんでした。日本の自己イメージは突如として変容したのです。

AKB48と芸能界の変化

「スーパースター」といえば、一般人に比べて**卓越**した才能と技能を持つ映画スターや音楽家を想像するかもしれません。彼らが住む世界は、ほとんどの人にとっては「手が届かない」ように見えることでしょう。しかし日本人は、あるスターたちのグループについては異なる基準を持っているようです。AKB48はその代表格であり、幅広いファン層を獲得し、優れたビジネスモデルを確立し、もしかすると日本の芸能界に変革をもたらすかもしれません。

17.1%, respectively. According to the Organization for Economic Co-operation and Development (OECD) reports, since 1985, the rate of child poverty in Japan increased to 14%, above the average of other OECD member nations.

Japan's population is growing older, and it is also declining. After **witnessing** the decline in job security, safety, chances for advancement, and a secure life after retirement, it was not difficult to understand how people started to let go of expectations, and even hope. Japanese had **clung to** the myth of the "middle-class nation," and had not recognized poverty as a relevant concept in Japan. Suddenly Japan's self-image was transformed.

AKB48 and Changes in the Entertainment Industry

When speaking of "superstars," one may imagine movie stars or musicians with **distinct** talent and skills beyond those of the ordinary person. The world they live in may seem "out of reach" for most people. But the Japanese people may have a different set of **criteria** for a particular group of stars. AKB48 is representative of that kind, winning a broad fan base and establishing a successful business model, and perhaps marking a change in the Japanese entertainment industry.

このポップグループは**広く知れ渡って**います。メンバーはポスターやテレビコマーシャルに登場し、その楽曲は多くのコンビニで流れています。彼女たちはブランドバッグを製作し、テレビ番組にレギュラーとして出演しています。しかし、彼女たちは秋葉原で活動するアマチュアグループとしてスタートし、多くの観客数を得ることもなく、「普通の女の子」のイメージを掲げていました——そしてこれが、彼女たちがいまも守る、成功のカギの一つなのです。「会いに行けるアイドル」として、彼女たちはソーシャルメディアや握手会など、ファンとのさまざまなやり取りを通じて、ファンを彼女たちの活動に「巻き込み」、**人気を博**しました。

　その究極の事例が、2018年まで行われていた「総選挙」です。このイベントでは、ファンの投票によって一番人気のメンバーが決まり、1位になったメンバーは次のシングルや公演で中心的なパフォーマーになりました。上位16位までのメンバーも、グループの次のシングルで歌う権利を手にしました。**投票用紙は**グループの最新シングルに封入されており、1人当たりの投票数に制限はないため、**熱心な**ファンはより多くのシングルを購入し、より多く投票することも可能です。これは公正な選挙のお手本とはいえませんが、マーケティング戦略としては成功しました。

　投票の過程で、ファンは、お気に入りのアイドルが育ち、成長していくことにかかわって

This pop group is **pervasive**: its members appear on posters and TV commercials, their songs are played in convenience stores, they fashion brand bags and appear as regulars on TV programs. However, they started out as an amateur group who performed in Akihabara and could not get more than a small audience, projecting a "girl-next-door" image—and this, they maintain, is one of the keys to their success. As "idols you could meet," they utilize social media, handshake events and other forms of interaction to "involve" fans in their activities and **boost their popularity**.

The ultimate example of this was their "election," which was held until 2018. Fans voted on the most popular member, who then became the central performer for the upcoming single and performances. The top 16 members also won their spots on the group's next single. The **ballots** are included in the group's latest single, and as there are no limits on the votes per person, **avid** fans can buy more singles to put in more votes. This is not an example of a fair election, but it proved successful as a marketing strategy.

Throughout the voting process, fans share a sense that they are taking part in their favorite idol's

いるという感覚を共有し、女の子たちが自分の妹や娘であるかのように、支持し、応援します。彼らは、あるメンバーがグループを「卒業」したり、何かのスキャンダルで「研究生」の身分に「降格」したりといったニュースに涙を流します。女の子たちがファンの生活の一部になるのです。メディア露出度とファン層は年々拡大しており、2013年の総選挙ではスタジアムが7万人の観衆で埋まり、6時間のテレビ生中継は平均20.3%の視聴率に達し、投票数は前年のほぼ倍の約260万票でした。

　AKB48のパフォーマンスと歌は、ほとんどジョークに見えるほど誇張に満ちています。しかしそのユーモアこそが、彼女たちのエンターテインメントのスタイルとパターンに特有のものであり、ファンもそれにお金を払っているのです。彼らはそのことをジョークのネタにもするし、ときにはけなしもしますが、それでも彼女たちを支持しているのです。彼女たちは素人っぽく、どこからともなくやってくるし、普通のルックスですが、それでも彼女たちの性格、背景、そして「努力」が一人ひとりの人気を呼ぶのです。ある意味において、AKB48は、スターの人生が、日本の若い女性の手の届かないところにあるわけではないことを証明したといえます。

　確かに、13歳のまだ幼い女の子が挑発的な衣装を身にまとって大胆な歌詞を歌い、アイドルとつながっているという誤ったイメージをファンに与えながら、実際には消費主義に

development and progress, and they support and cheer them on as if the girls are their little sisters or daughters. They cry at the news of particular members "graduating" from the group or being "**demoted**" **to** the "trainee" status due to some scandal. The girls become part of the fans' lives. The media coverage and fan base seem to grow each year, and the 2013 election filled a stadium with 70,000 **spectators,** the 6-hour live TV coverage reached an average of 20.3% **viewer rate,** and the number of votes almost doubled from the previous year, with **approximately** 2.6 million votes.

AKB48's performances and songs are full of **exaggeration,** which almost seem like jokes. But it is that humor that is characteristic of their entertainment style and culture, and fans buy into it. They joke about it, **bash** them at times, but support them. They have an amateurish style, **come out of nowhere,** and are average looking, but it is their character, background and the "effort" they show that win individual popularity. In a sense, AKB48 proved that the life of a star is not out of reach for any young woman in Japan.

Some criticize that it is **not appropriate** to have girls as young as 13 years old wear suggestive outfits and sing suggestive lyrics, and that they provide fans with a false sense of bonding with the idols, making them

基づいた関係に夢を抱かせるのは**不適切**だと批判する者もいます。しかし、このグループの人気は、大人の男性やオタクだけでなく、メンバーのファッションを追いかける若い女性や、彼女たちのようにアイドルになりたいと思っている、彼女たちよりもさらに幼い少女の間にも広がっているのです。また、2010年に「世界一人数の多いポップグループ」としてギネス世界記録に認定されました。そして、AKB48「本店」は、「支店」と呼ばれる姉妹グループや、AKB48の「公式」「非公式」のライバルグループ、またジャカルタ、上海などに拠点を置く国際版とともに、その後も躍進を続けました。

プロデューサーの秋元康は、アーティスト・グループをプロデュースしただけでなく、優れたビジネスモデルも確立しました。この**現象**は商業的側面を超えて、芸能界とともに日本の文化・社会を変える何かを**暗示しています**。この挑戦は、ビジネスモデルが型にはまり過ぎないようにし、**推進力と代謝作用**を維持することで、新旧のファンから興味と消費を引き出すものなのかもしれません。

常に変化しつつある日本の芸能界を反映して、別のグループの「会えるアイドル」(ただし「週末に」、というのも、ほとんどのメンバーが当時学生で、ほとんどのイベントやパフォーマンスが週末に開催されていたため)が登場しました。この「ももいろクローバーZ」とい

fantasize about their relationship while it is actually based on consumerism. However, the group has won popularity not just among adult men or *otaku* (the Japanese term for "geeks," or those who have strong passion about certain things, particularly anime and manga), but for young women who follow the members' fashion, and younger girls who want to be idols like them. Also, recognized by the Guinness World Records as the Largest Pop Group in 2010, the AKB48 franchise continued to grow, with spin-off sister groups, "official" or "unofficial rival groups of AKB48," and international versions, such as in Jakarta and Shanghai.

The producer, Akimoto Yasushi, has not only produced an artist group, but also established a successful business model. This **phenomenon** might go beyond commercial aspects and **imply** something about the changing entertainment industry, as well as culture and society in Japan. The challenge may be to prevent the business model from becoming too established, and keep the **momentum** and **metabolism** so they are fresh enough to attract interest and consumption from existing and new fans.

As a reflection of the changing Japanese entertainment industry, another group of "idols you can meet" ("on the weekends," since most were students at the time and held most of their events and performances on the weekends) appeared on the scene. Called Momoiro Clover Z, the 5-member group had a different style

う5人グループは、AKB48とは異なるスタイルで、**突飛な衣装を着て**、パフォーマンスにアクロバットや体操のようなアクションを組み合わせました。メンバーは、そのエネルギッシュなパフォーマンスでファンを**盛り上げ**、そのエネルギーとパワーで観客を楽しませ、希望を与えるのです。

　AKB48が、センター・ポジションを獲得するための競争と努力のグループだとすれば、ももいろクローバーZはパフォーマンスをより重視しており、その目指すところは大スターになることではなく、人々を楽しませることにあります。彼女たちが頑張っている姿を見ると、観衆に訴えかける小さなアマチュアバンドや劇団が思い浮かびます。もしかしたら、彼女たちの人気にはもう少し深い何かがあるのかもしれません——メンバーのエネルギーや躍動感を目の当たりにすることで、人々は、若かったころ、あるいは今、**精一杯生きている**だろうかと、思ったりするのかもしれません。彼女たちの**歌詞**やエネルギーは、若者だけではなく大人の心をもつかみ、辛いときに**耐える**元気を与えてくれるのです。

　背景にどのような事情や戦略があるにせよ、これらのグループの人気は、変化しつつある経済・社会に適応しようとする消費者のある種の新しい「ニーズ」を象徴しています。変化しないものの一つが音楽とエンターテインメントの力であり、人々の生活におけるその役割なのです。

from AKB48, incorporating **outrageous costumes** and action resembling acrobatics or gymnastics in their performances. The members **inspire** fans with their energetic performances, and their energy and power cheer audiences and give them hope.

While AKB48 is about competition and effort towards reaching a center position, Momoiro Clover Z is more about putting themselves into their performances, and their goal is not about becoming major stars but about entertaining people. Their efforts seem to remind people of a small amateur band or theatrical group, which also appeals to people. Perhaps their popularity means something a little deeper—witnessing the members' energy and drive, people may wonder if they lived their youth or are living their current lives **to the full**. Their **lyrics** and energy grabbed the hearts of adults, in addition to the younger fans, encouraging them to **endure** tough times.

Whatever exists in the background as reasons and strategies, the popularity of these groups seem to symbolize a new kind of consumer "need" to match the changing economy and society. One of the things that does not change is the power of music and entertainment, and its roles in people's lives.

3.11——地震、津波、そして原発災害

　2011年3月11日午後2時46分、東日本大震災として知られる大震災が発生しました。**震央**は、この地域の主要都市である仙台市の東の太平洋沖でした。地震は約6分間続き、当初はマグニチュード7.9と報告されました。その後、マグニチュードは9.0に引き上げられ、日本の史上最大規模、世界的にみても史上最大級の地震となりました。

　震央に最も近い都市は仙台市でしたが、強力な揺れは東北地方全域で感じられ、南は東京まで及びました。本震から30分でマグニチュード7以上の余震を3回記録し、住民をさらに不安に陥れました。**気象庁**は、体感された地震の揺れを表す独自の尺度（震度）を採用しています。この震度の最大値は7です。宮城県栗原市で最大震度の震度7が記録され、福島、茨城、栃木で震度6強、岩手、群馬、埼玉、千葉で震度6弱が記録されました。東京でも震度5強が観測されました。

　この地震は巨大な津波を引き起こし、東北地方の沿岸全域を襲いました。津波がこれほど大きな被害をもたらすとは、だれも想像していませんでした。海岸のあちらこちらに設けられた**防波堤**を津波がいとも簡単に乗り越えて

3.11 Earthquake, Tsunami and Nuclear Disaster

At 2:46 Japan Standard Time on March 11, 2011, an enormous earthquake which came to be known as the Great East Japan Earthquake struck. The **epicenter** was in the Pacific Ocean, east of Sendai, the region's largest city. The quake lasted about six minutes and was first reported as a magnitude 7.9. That measure was later raised to a magnitude 9.0, making the quake the largest in Japanese recorded history and one of the largest in recorded world history.

The city closest to the epicenter of the quake was Sendai, but enormous shaking was felt throughout northeast Japan and as far south as Tokyo. Within 30 minutes of the main quake, three more quakes with a magnitude of more than 7 followed, unsettling the populace further. The **Japan Meteorological Agency (JMA)** uses a separate scale to indicate the experienced ground motion of quakes. On this scale the maximum is 7. That maximum 7 was registered in Kurihara in Miyagi Prefecture, with an upper 6 in Fukushima, Ibaraki and Tochigi and a lower 6 in Iwate, Gunma, Saitama and Chiba. Even Tokyo was measured at an upper 5.

The earthquake triggered enormous tsunami that struck the entire northeast coast of the country. No one could imagine the damage that the tsunami would do. Video footage of tsunami easily rising over **seawalls** in port towns up and down the coast showed the barriers

いく様子を映した映像を見れば、そのような防壁が事実上無意味であったことがわかります。海水が防波堤を乗り越え、海岸だけでなく、内陸地域でも家屋、建物、車、船舶を破壊しました。岩手県宮古市では、津波の高さが40メートル近くに達したと推定されました。仙台では、地震から1時間後、津波が小さな防波堤を越えて低地の農地に流れ込んで少なくとも内陸4キロまで浸水し、農場、家屋、道路、鉄道、仙台空港の滑走路上の航空機が流されました。高台に避難しようとしていた住民は、津波がそれらの地域を襲った際、一緒に流されてしまいました。津波は太平洋も横断し、チリの海岸線2キロのところにまで到達しました。

　地震と津波という当初の災害だけでは不十分だとでもいうかのように、福島第一原子力発電所が損傷したことが明らかになり、さらなる懸念が持ち上がりました。海岸線沿いの施設を襲った津波は、そこに設置されていた4基の原子炉のうちの3基で、レベル7のメルトダウンを引き起こしました。原子炉損傷については1日に何度も新しいニュースが報じられましたが、数週間後まで実際の状況を確かめる方法がありませんでした。この間、政府は第一発電所の半径20キロメートル圏内の住民全員の避難を求めました。米国政府は、発電所から80キロメートル圏内の住民の避難を勧告しました。20万人以上が避難しました。

　首都圏の埋め立て地、特に東京都東部で、地震による液状化現象が生じました。

to be virtually useless. Water gushed over the tops of the walls, destroying houses, buildings, cars and boats not only on the edge of the water but deep inland as well. At Miyako in Iwate Prefecture, the height of the tsunami was estimated at close to 40 meters (133 feet). At Sendai, an hour after the quake, a tsunami flooded over minimal breakwaters into low-lying farm land and pushed up to at least 4 kilometers inland, sweeping away farms, houses, roads, railways, and planes on the tarmac at Sendai Airport. People who rushed for higher ground were carried away when the water swept over those sites. Tsunami also raced across the Pacific as well, reaching 2 kilometers along the coast of Chile.

As if the initial damage of the quake and the tsunami were not bad enough, further concerns were raised when it became known that the Fukushima Daiichi **Nuclear Power Plant complex** has suffered damage. The tsunami that struck the shoreline **facility** caused a level 7 meltdown at three of the four **reactors** located there. News about the damage to the nuclear reactors was updated several times a day, although there was no way to confirm the actual situation until weeks later. **In the meantime**, the government called for the **evacuation** of all residents within a 20 kilometer radius of the Daiichi plant. The U.S. government recommended the evacuation of its citizens up to 80 kilometers from the plant. Over 200,000 people were evacuated.

The quake also caused **soil liquefaction** in areas where land had been reclaimed in the Tokyo area,

三重災害による**犠牲者数**と損害の推定は困難な状況が続きました。1万6000人近くが複合災害で死亡し、さらに6000人以上が負傷、約3000人が行方不明になりました。南三陸などは、全町が壊滅しました。

　震災直後、地震と福島原発の損傷による電力不足のため、**停電が繰り返されました**。地震によって東北沿岸部の原子炉11基が**自動停止しました**。電力不足に追い打ちをかけたのが、地震によって発生した千葉と仙台の**製油所**での火災でした。東北地方の高速道路と鉄道は当初完全に停止し、段階的に復旧するほかなく、援助や救助はなかなか進みませんでした。被災地の電話は、深刻な途絶状態が何日も続きました。

　大規模な宗教団体や外国政府は、さまざまな方法で犠牲者を救済するための資金、**装備**、必需品を供出し、ボランティアを派遣しました。**自然発生的な**ボランティアのグループは、夜に被災地入りし、一日を費やして**がれき類**を片付けたり、**排水溝の泥をシャベルですく**い出したりした後、その日遅く帰宅しました。

　災害によって発生した長期的問題は**多様**でした。第1に、自分の家、愛する者、そして着ているもの以外、実質的にすべてを失った人々が、ともかくまだ崩れていないだけの建物のなかで**身を寄せ合っていました**。しかし、彼らには食糧も、水も、暖房器具も、医療支援もありませんでした。数週間がたち、これらの

notably the eastern wards of the city.

It remained difficult to estimate the **casualties** and the damage caused by the **three-pronged disaster**. Close to 16,000 died in the combined disaster, with more than 6,000 more injured, and almost 3,000 missing. Entire towns like Minami Sanriku were destroyed.

In the aftermath, **there were rolling blackouts** due to power shortages caused by the quake and the destruction of the nuclear plants in Fukushima. Eleven reactors on the Tohoku coast **were automatically shut down** by the quake. Complicating the power shortage were fires started by the quake at **refineries** in Chiba and in Sendai. Highways and train lines in Tohoku were completely shut down initially and only reopened step by step, which hindered aid and rescue efforts. Phone service in the affected areas was seriously disrupted for days.

Large religious groups and foreign governments donated funds, **equipment**, supplies and volunteer time to help the victims in various ways. **Spontaneous** groups of volunteers traveled to disaster areas at night, put in a day clearing **debris** or shoveling mud out of **drains**, and then returned home late in the day.

The long-term problems created by the disaster were **multiple**. First, people who had lost their homes, their loved ones and virtually everything but their clothes **huddled** in whatever buildings remained standing. But they had no food, no water, no heat and no medical aid. As weeks wore on, some of them were transported to other regions temporarily. They

物資の一部が一時的にほかの地域に運ばれました。住民は生活を再開するための支援を必要としていました。戻るべき学校も病院も職場もなかったからです。その間、彼らは高台の平地に急造された仮設住宅で暮らしました。

第2に、津波による海水や、また福島県では**放射能汚染**によって、農地が被害を受けました。福島第一原発の環境汚染が制御できるようになるまで、いわゆる「除染作業」すら着手できませんでした。この施設を完全に制御できるようになるまで、数十年を要すると推定されました。漁業は東北のもう一つの主要産業でしたが、ほぼ完全に**消滅**しました。船舶は沈没もしくは損傷し、漁港はがれきであふれ、養殖場は津波によって全滅しました。第3に、被災地のほとんどは、すでに人口減少と高齢化に苦しんでいました。高齢被害者はしばしば帰宅を強く望んでいましたが、彼らの子や孫たちは帰宅することにほとんど重きを置きませんでした。

竹島と尖閣諸島をめぐる領土問題

北海道東海岸に位置するいわゆる「北方領土」に関し、ロシアとの不一致打開の進展がほとんどないなか、日本はほかの国々と2つの諸島をめぐる**論争**において、さらに複雑な問題に直面しました。

needed help to restart their lives, because there were no schools, hospitals or workplaces to return to. In the meantime, they occupied quickly-built temporary housing constructed in available flat lands in the higher areas.

Second, farmland was damaged by saltwater from the tsunami and, in Fukushima, by **nuclear contamination**. So-called "clean-up operations" could not even be commenced until the environmental hazard at Fukushima Daiichi could be put under control. Complete control of that facility was estimated as taking several decades. Fishing, the other major industry of the northeast, was almost completely **wiped out**. Boats were sunk or destroyed, ports were filled with debris, and fisheries were wiped out by the tsunami. Third, most of the affected areas were already suffering a population decline and advanced aging. Though aged victims were often eager to return home, their children and grandchildren found little value in trying to return.

Territorial Dispute over Takeshima and Senkaku Islands

While Japan continued to make little progress toward solving its disagreements with Russia over the so-called "Northern Territories" off the east coast of Hokkaido, it faced even more complex problems in **disputes** with other countries over two different groups of islands.

東シナ海では、中国で魚釣島と呼ばれる尖閣諸島の領有権をめぐり中国と**対立しました**。2010年、中国の漁船が日本の巡視艇に追跡され、尖閣諸島から遠くない海域で巡視艇に追突しました。巡視艇は漁船とその船長、船員を拿捕しました。中国の各都市ではこの行為に対する抗議行動が起こり、日系企業は深刻な被害を受けました。最終的には船員は釈放され、船も返還されています。

　やがて、どちらの国が実際に尖閣諸島に対するより強い権利を有しているかについては、両国とも**発言を弱める**ようになりました。これらの島々には、基本的に人は住めませんが、支配する国の排他的な経済的権利を保証するものであるため非常に重要な島々なのです。8つの島と**岩礁島**の海底には膨大な油田とガス田があるとみられているため、**利害が大きい**のです。元東京都知事の石原慎太郎は2012年、個人所有の3島を東京都が購入する意志があると発言し、再び緊張が高まりました。翌年、日本の文部科学省が、問題の島々を日本領土とする地理と政治経済の教科書を検定合格とした際、中国政府が抗議しました。

　もう一つの白熱した問題は竹島です。この島は日本海にあり韓国が支配する岩礁の集まりで、韓国では独島、第三国ではリアンクール岩礁として知られています。ここでの問題もまた、小さな島々の周辺の海洋資源の権利にかかわるものです。この問題は、領土問題とい

In the East China Sea, Japan **squared off with** China over claims to the Senkaku Islands, which the Chinese call the Diaoyu Islands. In 2010 a Chinese fishery vessel being pursued by a Japanese Coast Guard vessel rammed the Japanese ship not far from the waters of these islands. The Japanese vessel seized the boat, its captain and its crew. Massive protests broke out in Chinese cities against this action, with damage done to Japanese-owned businesses. Eventually the crew and ship were released.

In time, both sides **cooled the rhetoric** over which country actually has the strongest claim to the islands. Although fundamentally uninhabitable, these islands are extremely valuable for the exclusive economic rights they guarantee to the nation that controls them. The eight islands and **rocky islets** are thought to sit atop vast oil and gas reserves, so the **stakes** are high. When former Tokyo Governor Ishihara Shintaro in 2012 stated his intention to have Tokyo buy three of the privately owned islands, tensions reheated. The following year the Chinese government protested when the Japanese education ministry approved textbooks in geography and politics and economics claiming the disputed islands as Japanese territories.

Another heated issue involved Takeshima, a South Korea—administered chain of islets in the Sea of Japan, known in Korean as the Dokdo Islands and elsewhere as the Liancourt Rocks. The issue here, too, is over rights to resources in the seas around the small islands. This dispute is not so much a territorial issue as a

うよりはむしろ、歴史的な記憶と**解釈**の問題
です。両国の漁業組合はこの島の周辺海域を
共有することで合意しようとしました。しか
し、どちらの国が島を実際に所有しているの
かを議論するばかりで、進展はほとんどみら
れませんでした。

アベノミクス

　自由民主党の政治家、安倍晋三は、2006年
から2007年にかけて最初に首相を務めた際、
散々な経験をしました。安倍首相が早期退陣
した後、日本の首相はめまぐるしく替わること
となり、数十年の歴史のなかで初めて民主党
の代表が首相になったこともありました。し
かし、いずれの指導者も有効な経済政策を**実
行する**ことができず、日本の20年の**デフレ不
況**が続きました。2011年3月11日（東日本大
震災）以降、状況の好転はさらに難しくなりま
した。

　思いもよらないことが起きたのは、2012年
12月、安倍が自民党を率いて**総選挙**で圧勝を
収め、再び首相に返り咲いたときのことです。
半年後、安倍は、それまでの8人の首相のだれ
よりも高い支持率を得ることとなり、だれもが
「アベノミクス」という新語を口にするように
なったのです。

　安倍は3本柱の計画を導入して、日本がなか

matter of historical memory and **interpretation**. Fishing communities in the two countries sought to reach an agreement to share the waters around the island. But little progress was made in discussing who actually owned the islands.

Abenomics

LDP politician Abe Shinzo made a miserable showing in his first visit to the office of prime minister in 2006–2007. His early departure from office was followed by a revolving door of faces, including, for the first time in decades, representatives of the Democratic Party of Japan. None of these leaders, however, was able to **implement** economic policies that worked, and Japan's 20-year **deflationary recession** continued. Positive change became even more difficult after March 11, 2011.

The unexpected happened when Abe won leadership of his party, led the LDP to a **landslide victory** in the **general election** of December 2012, and returned to the post of prime minister. Six months later he enjoyed a higher approval rating than any of the eight previous prime ministers and a new word was added to everyone's vocabulary: Abenomics.

Abe introduced a three-pronged plan to end the

なか抜け出せなかった長いデフレ不況に終止符を打とうとしました。この「3本の矢」の計画とは、大胆な**金融刺激策**、財政政策、グローバルな競争と成長を促進する**構造改革**を指します。この3本目の「矢」には、**先端産業を創出**し、企業競争を促進して、外国からの投資を呼び込むねらいがありました。

　最初の2本の「矢」は、世間やメディアにとても良い印象を与えたようで、「アベノミクス」は日本国内の事実上すべての好ましい兆しの要因であると考えられるようになりました。日本の株式市場は半年間で80％の回復を見せ、2012年11月には9000円前後だった日経平均株価（日経225）は、2013年5月には1万5000円前後まで上昇しました。日本株の株主は株価上昇を喜びましたが、それが円安を招き、日本円は1米ドルが100円以上となりました。海外における日本製品の販売が順調になる一方、原油などの輸入品の価格は高騰しました。

COVID-19感染爆発が変えた日常生活

　2度目となった東京オリンピックは新型コロナウイルス（COVID-19）の**感染爆発**により開催延期となり、新たな日程が決まっても、**急速化**する感染拡大にもかかわらず多くの選手や観光客が来日することに対する懸念の声が高まりました。しかし最終的には、オリンピッ

long deflationary slump that Japan has been unable to escape. The "three arrows" of this plan were massive **monetary stimulus**, fiscal stimulus, and **structural reforms** to spur global competitiveness and growth. This last "arrow" aimed at creating **cutting-edge industry**, promoting competition between businesses, and attracting foreign investors.

The first two "arrows" seemed to impress the public and the media so much that "Abenomics" came to be seen as the cause for virtually all positive signs in Japan. The Japanese stock market made a recovery of some 80% in six months, with the Nikkei 225 climbing from around 9,000 in November 2012 to around 15,000 in May of 2013. Holders of Japanese stocks were happy to see their stocks rise, but that significantly weakened the yen to over 100 yen to the U.S. dollar at one point. While it was much easier to sell Japanese goods overseas, the cost of oil and other imports rose significantly.

Covid pandemic changes daily life

Due to the COVID-19 **pandemic**, Tokyo's second hosting of the Olympic Games was postponed, and once the dates were reset, there was great concern about the impact of significant numbers of athletes and visitors coming into the country despite **spikes** in the spread of the disease. In the end, however, both the Olympics and

ク、パラリンピックとも成功を収めました。

　感染爆発は、日本社会のあらゆる領域に広範な影響をもたらしました。感染拡大防止のために学校は閉鎖され、小学生から大学生まで、**リモート学習**に対応せざるをえなくなりました。そのため教師たちも、コンピューターやタブレット端末を利用したまったく新しい方法に適応しなければならなくなりました。自宅で画面を見つめていても、生徒が教師に助言を求める機会はさほど多くなく、授業の合間に**クラスメートとおしゃべりをする**時間もありません。後の研究によれば、この期間中に学習水準が世界的にやや低下し、生徒たちの**孤立感**、人間関係への自信の喪失がみられました。

　感染爆発は日本の労働文化にも大きな影響を与えました。長時間労働、**対面の会議**、そして常に上司が監督しているという特徴を持つ日本の労働文化は、リモートワークへの転換によって大きく揺らぎました。社員は自宅や喫茶店から**オンラインで業務を行い**、与えられた仕事を明確にしたり、上司に確認したり、クライアントに対応したりすることが難しくなりました。

　毎日ではないにせよ**在宅勤務**が急増し、過剰残業の可能性が減り、対面でのやり取りがなくなりました。管理職は、オフィスに来ない従業員の業務分担と**進捗状況の確認**のため、新たな方法を模索しなければならなくなりました。従業員は、仕事についての同僚との相談

Paralympics were a success.

The pandemic had a widespread impact on Japanese society at many levels. Schools closed to prevent the spread of the disease, forcing students from elementary through to college age to adapt to **remote learning**. This forced teachers to teach in entirely new ways, using computers or tablets. Staring at a screen at home did not give students as many opportunities to ask teachers for help, nor did students have as much time for **chatting** with classmates between lessons. Researchers later found that learning levels declined slightly worldwide during that period, and it left students **feeling isolated** and less confident in personal relationships.

The pandemic also impacted Japan's work culture significantly. Known for long office hours, **in-person meetings**, and visible manager oversight, Japanese work culture was shaken by major shifts to remote work. With employees **carrying out their duties online** from home or a coffee shop, it was difficult for them to clarify their assigned tasks, check with their supervisors, and deal with clients.

Telecommuting at least part of each week increased rapidly, reducing the option of excessive overtime and eliminating face-to-face interactions. With workers not coming to the office, managers had to adjust to other ways of dividing tasks and **monitoring progress**. Workers were not able to consult with coworkers regarding

や、アイデアの共有ができなくなり、多くの従業員が孤立し、意欲の低下につながりました。

　託児所や学校が閉鎖されたため、子育て中の従業員は**困難に直面し**、自宅で子どもの面倒を見ながら、自分の仕事をリモートで、同じ家、同じ部屋でこなそうとしました。

　反面で、会社勤めの人々のなかには、オフィス閉鎖により、満員電車やバスを乗り継いで通勤しなくてもよくなった人もいます。多くの人が、通勤にいかに多くの時間とエネルギーを費やしていたかに気づきました。在宅勤務は睡眠時間の増加、オフィスにおける人間関係のストレス軽減、運動機会の増加さえ、もたらしたのです。

　フルタイムでオフィスとバーチャルに接続できるようになったことから、一部の会社員は、一時的に、あるいは完全に地方に**移住しました**。インターネットに接続できる場所ならどこでもよく、こうした人々には、感染爆発が収束していくなかで、すべての従業員をオフィスに呼び戻すという企業の方針は**不評**でした。

　一般的な日本人は**ワクチン接種**など予防策を講じていますが、感染爆発の際のオフィス閉鎖の影響は今も続いています。日本の伝統的なビジネススタイルに完全に戻る可能性は限定的です。

assignments or share ideas with one another. Many employees felt isolated and unengaged.

With daycare centers and schools closed, workers with children **were in a real pinch**, having to tend to their homebound children's needs and trying to get their own jobs done remotely, in the same house, or even in the same room.

The flip side of this was that for some office workers, not having to commute on crowded trains and buses to their workplaces was a positive result of the shutting down of offices. Many realized how much time and energy they had previously devoted to just getting to and from the office each day. Working from home allowed more sleep, less stress from office politics, and even more chances to get some exercise.

Some employees who could connect virtually with the office on a full-time basis **relocated** temporarily or permanently to the countryside. Any place with an internet connection was sufficient. For this group, as the pandemic subsided, some companies' decisions to call all of their workers back to the office were **unwelcome**.

The impact of the shutdown of offices during the pandemic continues to be felt despite the **vaccinations** and the other precautions that the average Japanese takes. The chances of a complete return to the "traditional Japanese way" of doing business are limited.

天皇の退位

　近年の歴史では、新天皇が**即位する**のは前の天皇の死後です。しかし2019年5月、明仁天皇は高齢と体力の衰えを理由に**退位しました**。長男である徳仁親王が第126代天皇として即位し、その治世は「令和」と名付けられました。同年10月22日、神職と**侍従**のみが参列する厳かな儀式で正式に即位した新天皇は、伝統と期待に縛られた世界に足を踏み入れました。

　皇室に焦点が当てられると、女性皇族の皇位継承権の可否問題が再び浮上しました。1947年に制定された皇室典範によれば、皇位継承権は**直系男子**にあります。現在、皇位継承者は2人しかいません。秋篠宮親王は58歳（2023年現在）、彼の息子の悠仁親王は17歳です。

　ほかの懸念もあります。皇室の縮小に伴い——女性皇族は**一般人**と結婚すると皇族の身分を放棄しなければならない——皇族が現在の公務をすべてこなすことが難しくなっています。東日本大震災での避難者訪問、慈善事業の名誉会長、学校訪問、年中行事の遂行、**外国要人**の迎接など、残された皇族の公務は多岐にわたっています。

The Emperor's abdication

In recent history, a new emperor has **taken the throne** only after the death of his predecessor. But in May 2019, Emperor Akihito **abdicated** due to his age and infirmity. His eldest son, Prince Naruhito, became the 126th emperor of Japan, and his reign was given the name "Reiwa." Officially enthroned on October 22 that year in elaborate rituals observed only by Shinto priests and **chamberlains**, the new emperor entered a world that remains bound by tradition and expectations.

Focus on the **imperial family** once again brought up the issue of whether its female members might one day succeed to the throne. According to the 1947 Imperial House Law, only **direct male descendants** are in the line of accession. Currently there are only two in line: Crown Prince Akishino, at 58 (as of 2023), is followed by his son Prince Hisahito, at 17.

There are additional concerns: as the imperial family shrinks—because female members are required to give up their royal status when they marry **commoners**—it has become difficult for members to manage all of their current official duties. Visiting evacuees following the 2011 Tohoku earthquake and tsunami, serving as honorary chairpersons of charities, visiting schools, carrying out annual rituals, and greeting **foreign dignitaries** are among the duties that remaining members are called on to carry out.

安倍晋三暗殺とその余波

　日本で最も長期にわたって首相を務めた安倍晋三は、2022年7月8日に奈良市で行われた選挙演説中に**暗殺されました**。安倍は2020年に首相を辞しましたが、自由民主党の**重鎮**であり続けました。

　首相在任中、安倍は**憲法改正**、国際社会における日本の立場の強化、防衛予算の増加、教科書の**国粋主義的**な内容への改訂、そして低迷する経済の立て直しを図るなどにより、多くの反対に直面していました。しかし暗殺者・山上徹也にとって、これらの問題は動機ではありませんでした。

　山上は捜査当局に対し、彼の標的は元首相ではなく、(旧)統一教会総裁の韓鶴子だったと述べました。彼女に近づくことができなかったため、山上は教会と「深い関係」を持つと信じる安倍を**射殺する**ことに決めました。安倍は祖父(岸信介元首相)の代からの統一教会とのつながりを維持していました。同教会とのつながりは、時に「ムーニー」と呼ばれることもあります。

　山上は自身の母親が統一教会に多額の寄付を強いられ、家族に**借金を背負わせた**と主張します。その結果、彼の父と兄は自殺したと思い、山上自身も自殺を図ったことがありました。

The assassination of Abe Shinzo and its aftermath

Abe Shinzo, Japan's longest-serving prime minister, was in Nara giving a campaign speech on a street corner in support of a local candidate when he **was assassinated** on July 8, 2022. Abe had given up the post of prime minister in 2020, but he remained a **central force** within the ruling Liberal Democratic Party (LDP).

As prime minister, Abe had faced strong opposition for his moves to **revise the constitution,** to have Japan assert itself in the world, to increase defense spending, to rewrite school textbooks so that they were more **nationalistic**, and to somehow regenerate Japan's sluggish economy. But none of these issues was a motivation for the assassin, Yamagami Tetsuya.

Yamagami told investigators that his prime target was not the former prime minister but the Unification Church's top official, Hak Ja Han. Unable to **gain access to** her, Yamagami decided to **shoot** Abe, whom he believed to be "deeply connected" to the Church. Abe had maintained his grandfather's (Prime Minister Kishi Nobusuke's) connection with the group, which is sometimes referred to as the "Moonies."

Yamagami claimed that his mother had been heavily pressured to donate enormous sums of money to the group, **putting** her own family **deep into debt**. Yamagami believed that as a result, his father and brother had

この暗殺事件は日本国民に大きな衝撃を与えました。日本ではこのような暗殺は考えられないと広く思い込まれていたこともあって、警備は明らかに不十分でした。この認識は、2023年4月に岸田文雄首相への暗殺**未遂事件**が発生したことで、誤りであることが再び示されました。

安倍暗殺事件の捜査は大きな反響を呼び起こしました。統一教会とその集金方法、特に**霊感商法**と会員に対する直接的な献金の強要について、長期にわたる幅広い**マスコミの報道**が明るみに出ました。多くの政治家がこの団体と関わりを持っていたことから、警察とメディアによる広範な捜査につながりました。この暗殺事件がなければ、こうした事態は発生しなかったでしょう。

大谷翔平が世界的スーパースターに

大谷翔平が日本プロ野球（NPB）から23歳で米ロサンゼルスを拠点とするエンゼルスに移籍した際、何を期待してよいものか、ほとんど不透明でした。日本での5シーズンを終え、彼は類まれな**才能**の持ち主であることを証明していました。しかし、メジャーリーグで投

both committed suicide, and he had attempted suicide once himself.

The assassination was a shock to the Japanese. Security measures had obviously failed, in part due to the fundamental belief that such assassinations could not happen in Japan. That assumption was once again proven false by an **unsuccessful attempt** on the life of Prime Minister Kishida in April 2023.

The investigation into the assassination of Abe had broad repercussions. It brought to light long-term, widespread **media coverage** of the Unification Church and its ruthless methods of raising money from "**spiritual sales**" and then pressuring members for direct donations. The fact that many politicians were associated with this group led to a broad investigation by police and the media. None of this would have occurred had the assassination incident not occurred.

Ohtani Shohei becomes a worldwide superstar

When Ohtani Shohei left Japan's Nippon Professional Baseball (NPB) at age 23 and began playing for the Los Angeles Angels in 2018, few observers knew what to expect. After five seasons in Japan, he had proven he was a **singular talent**. But could he be an elite pitcher-hitter phenomenon in the Major Leagues?

手兼打者として、果たして成功するだろうか、と。

　彼はすぐに「二刀流」の選手として、マウンドとバッターボックスの両方で**卓越した能力**を示しました。最初に比較されたのは、1920年代初頭にニューヨーク・ヤンキースで活躍したベーブ・ルースだけでした。しかし2018年9月、大谷は初めて右肘の内側側副靭帯を**損傷しました**。打つことはできましたが、残りのシーズンと翌シーズンは投げることができませんでした。2020年の新型コロナによって短縮されたシーズン中に、投手として2シーズン出場したときは苦しみました。

　しかし2021年には**驚異的な進化を遂げ**、一流打者・投手としての名声をものにしました。シーズン終了時にはMVP（最優秀選手）に選出されました。ヤンキースのアーロン・ジャッジが62本塁打で長年のアメリカン・リーグ記録を破っていなければ、翌年も同賞を受賞していたでしょう。

　2023年、大谷はワールド・ベースボール・クラシック（WBC）で日本を**優勝に導き**、レギュラーシーズンでも本塁打数と投手としてトップの成績を収めました。そして2023年、シーズンを2カ月残して再び**手術**が必要になりました。それにもかかわらず、2度目のMVPに選ばれました。

　彼の特筆すべき点は、史上最高の**野球選手**になることに強いこだわりを持ちつつ、**親しみやすい人柄**だということです。あらゆる世代、

He quickly proved that he could be a *ni-to ryu* (two-way) player, **excelling** on the mound and in the batter's box. The only player that was initially offered as a comparison was the New York Yankee's Babe Ruth in the early 1920s. But in September 2018 Ohtani **tore** the ulnar collateral ligament in his right elbow for the first time. He was still able to hit, but he was unable to pitch for the rest of that season and the following one. When he pitched in two seasons during the Covid-shortened season of 2020, he struggled.

But in 2021 he **made a breakthrough**, becoming an elite batter and pitcher who exceeded all expectations. At season's end, he was selected as MVP (most valuable player). He would have received the same award the following year, had it not been for the Yankees' Aaron Judge breaking a long-standing American League record with 62 home runs.

In 2023 Ohtani **led** the Japanese team **to victory** in the World Baseball Classic, and continued the regular season at the top of the charts in home runs and as a pitcher. Then he needed **surgery** again in 2023, with two months left in the season. Despite that, he was selected as MVP a second time.

What made Ohtani unique was that although he was strongly dedicated to becoming the best **ballplayer** of all time, he was highly **personable**. People of all ages

国の人々が彼を称賛しました。他球団を敵地で**破って**も、ファンは、2023年にエンゼルスとの契約が終了したら移籍してきてほしいと声を上げました。メディアを**騒然と**させた後、大谷はロサンゼルス・ドジャースと契約しました。

　大谷の「史上最高の選手になる」という**野心**、常に技術を向上させようとする献身的な姿勢、そして**人懐っこさ**は、日米だけでなく、プロ野球界の枠を超えて人気を博しています。

and all nations admired him. Even if he was **defeating** another team at their home stadium, the fans chanted their hopes that he would transfer to their club when his contract with the Angels came to an end in 2023. Following a media **frenzy** around his career move, he signed with the Los Angeles Dodgers.

Ohtani's **ambition** to be the best *of all time*, his complete dedication to constantly improving his skills, and his general **affability** made him popular well beyond Japan and the United States, and well beyond the world of professional baseball.

参 考 資 料

Appendix

日本現代史略年表
A Brief Chronology of Contemporary Japanese History

1945 (昭和20)	ポツダム宣言受諾、終戦 Acceptance of terms of the Potsdam Declaration, end of war	鈴木貫太郎 Suzuki Kantaro
	玉音放送 Imperial radio broadcast announcing end of hostilities	
	マッカーサー来日 General MacArthur arrives in Japan	東久邇宮稔彦王 Higashikuni Naruhiko
	GHQの占領政策はじまる（財閥解体・農地改革） SCAP headquarters commences occupation policies (dissolution of financial combines, reform of agricultural land)	幣原喜重郎 Shidehara Kijuro
1946 (昭和21)	天皇の人間宣言 Emperor renounces divinity	
	第1次公職追放はじまる Commencement of first purge of public leaders	
	極東国際軍事裁判（東京裁判）開廷 Opening of International Military Tribunal for the Far East (Tokyo Trial)	
	日本国憲法発布 Constitution of Japan promulgated	吉田茂（第1次） Yoshida Shigeru (1st term)
	チャーチル「鉄のカーテン演説」／冷戦の幕開け Winston Churchill's Iron Curtain speech / Beginning of the Cold War	
1947 (昭和22)	GHQ、二・一ストを禁止 GHQ bans General Strike of 1947	
	日本国憲法施行 Constitution of Japan goes into effect	片山哲 Katayama Tetsu
1948 (昭和23)	経済安定九原則公布 Issuance of the Nine Principles for Economic Stabilization	芦田均 Ashida Hitoshi
	大韓民国・朝鮮民主主義人民共和国成立 Establishment of Republic of Korea & Democratic People's Republic of Korea	吉田茂（第2次） Yoshida Shigeru (2nd term)
1949 (昭和24)	ドッジ＝ライン／1ドル＝360円の為替レートに Dodge Line / Establishment of constant exchange rate of US $1 to ¥360	吉田茂（第3次） Yoshida Shigeru (3rd term)
	下山事件・三鷹事件・松川事件 Shimoyama Incident, Mitaka Incident, Matsukawa Incident	

	湯川秀樹ノーベル物理学賞受賞 Yukawa Hideki receives Nobel Prize for physics	
	中華人民共和国成立 People's Republic of China established	
1950（昭和25）	レッドパージ（第2次公職追放）はじまる Red Purge, second purge of government employees begins	
	警察予備隊令公布 National Police Reserve directive promulgated	
1951（昭和26）	サンフランシスコ講和条約・日米安全保障条約調印 San Francisco Peace Treaty & United States–Japan Security Treaty signed	
1952（昭和27）	サンフランシスコ講和条約・日米安全保障条約発効 San Francisco Peace Treaty & United States–Japan Security Treaty go into effect	
	破壊活動防止法公布 Subversive Activities Prevention Law promulgated	吉田茂（第4次） Yoshida Shigeru (4th term)
	警察予備隊、保安隊に改編 National Police Reserve reorganized as National Safety Forces	
1953（昭和28）	テレビ放送はじまる Beginning of television broadcasting in Japan	吉田茂（第5次） Yoshida Shigeru (5th term)
	水俣病、第1号患者報告される First case of Minamata disease reported	
1954（昭和29）	第5福竜丸事件 Lucky Dragon Incident	
	自衛隊発足 Establishment of Self Defense Forces	鳩山一郎（第1次） Hatoyama Ichiro (1st term)
1955（昭和30）	第1回原水爆禁止世界大会、広島で開催 First Atomic Disasters Anniversary World Conference held in Hiroshima	鳩山一郎（第2・3次） Hatoyama Ichiro (2nd, 3rd terms)
1956（昭和31）	日ソ共同宣言 Soviet–Japan Joint Declaration	
	日本、国際連合加盟 Japan become member of United Nations	石橋湛山 Ishibashi Tanzan
1957（昭和32）		岸信介（第1・2次） Kishi Nobusuke (1st, 2nd terms)

1958（昭和33）		
1959（昭和34）		
1960（昭和35）	新安保条約調印 Second of the United States–Japan security treaties signed	
	日本社会党委員長・浅沼稲次郎、刺殺される Asanuma Inejiro, chairman of Japan Socialist Party, assassinated	池田勇人（第1・2次） Ikeda Hayato (1st, 2nd terms)
1961（昭和36）		
1962（昭和37）	キューバ危機 Cuban missile crisis	
1963（昭和38）	ケネディ大統領暗殺 President Kennedy assassinated	池田勇人（第3次） Ikeda Hayato (3rd term)
1964（昭和39）	東京オリンピック開催 Tokyo Olympic Games held	佐藤栄作（第1次） Sato Eisaku (1st term)
1965（昭和40）	日韓基本条約調印 Korea–Japan Treaty signed	
	ベ平連（ベトナムに平和を市民連合）、最初のデモ Peace for Vietnam Committee holds first demonstration against the Vietnam War	
	米軍の北爆開始 American bombardment of North Vietnam begins	
1966（昭和41）	中国で文化大革命はじまる Cultural Revolution begins in China	
1967（昭和42）	非核三原則を示す Three non-nuclear principles published	佐藤栄作（第2次） Sato Eisaku (2nd term)
1968（昭和43）	大学紛争はじまる University upheavals begin	
	小笠原諸島返還 Ogasawara Islands return to Japanese sovereignty	
	川端康成ノーベル文学賞受賞 Kawabata Yasunari receives Nobel Prize for literature	
1969（昭和44）	佐藤・ニクソン共同声明／1972年の沖縄返還合意 Sato–Nixon Communiqué / Agreement on reversion of Okinawa to Japanese sovereignty in 1972	
1970（昭和45）	大阪で万博開催 Expo '70 opens in Osaka	佐藤栄作（第3次） Sato Eisaku (3rd term)

	「よど号」事件 Yodo-go Incident	
	三島由紀夫事件 Mishima Yukio commits suicide	
1971 (昭和46)	ドル・ショック／円切り上げ (1ドル＝308円) "Dollar shock" / Japanese yen reevaluated at $1 to ¥308	
1972 (昭和47)	連合赤軍あさま山荘事件 United Red Army Asama Lodge Incident	
	日中共同声明／日中国交回復 China–Japan Joint Communiqué / Restoration of diplomatic relations between People's Republic of China and Japan	田中角栄 (第1・2次) Tanaka Kakuei (1st, 2nd terms)
	変動相場制に移行 Floating exchange rate introduced	
1973 (昭和48)	オイルショック Oil crisis	
	ベトナム和平協定調印 Agreement on Restoring the Peace in Vietnam signed	
1974 (昭和49)		三木武夫 Miki Takeo
1976 (昭和51)	ロッキード事件 Lockheed scandal	
	天安門事件 Tiananmen Square Incident	福田赳夫 Fukuda Takeo
	南北ベトナム統一 North and South Vietnam unified	
1977 (昭和52)		
1978 (昭和53)	日中平和友好条約調印 China–Japan Peace and Friendship Treaty signed	
	日米防衛協力のための指針 (ガイドライン) 決定 Guidelines set for Japan-United States defense cooperation	大平正芳 (第1・2次) Ohira Masayoshi (1st, 2nd terms)
1979 (昭和54)	ソ連、アフガニスタン侵攻 Soviet Union invades Afghanistan	
1980 (昭和55)	イラン・イラク戦争 Iran–Iraq War	鈴木善幸 Suzuki Zenko
1981 (昭和56)	中国残留孤児が初来日 First visit to Japan of displaced Japanese war orphans from China	
1982 (昭和57)		中曽根康弘 (第1・2次) Nakasone Yasuhiro (1st, 2nd terms)

1983（昭和58）		
1984（昭和59）		
1985（昭和60）	日航機ジャンボジェット墜落 Crash of JAL jumbo jet	
1986（昭和61）	男女雇用機会均等法成立 Equal Employment Opportunity Law for Men and Women enacted	
	チェルノブイリ原発事故 Chernobyl nuclear accident	中曾根康弘（第3次） Nakasone Yasuhiro (3rd term)
1987（昭和62）	国鉄分割・民営化 Breakup and privatization of Japan National Railway	
		竹下登 Takeshita Noboru
1988（昭和63）	リクルート事件 Recruit scandal	
1989（昭和64・平成元年）	昭和天皇崩御、平成と改元 Death of Emperor Showa, beginning of the Heisei era	
	消費税3％でスタート Consumption tax of 3% goes into effect	
	第2次天安門事件 Second Tiananmen Square Incident	宇野宗佑 Uno Sosuke
	ベルリンの壁崩壊 Berlin Wall demolished	海部俊樹（第1・2次） Kaifu Toshiki (1st, 2nd terms)
1990（平成2）	天皇明仁、正式に即位 Emperor Akihito formally enthroned	
	イラク、クエートに侵攻／湾岸戦争はじまる Iraq invades Kuwait / Persian Gulf War begins	
	東西ドイツ統一 East and West Germany unified	
1991（平成3）	イラク空爆開始 Commencement of bombing of Iraq	
	ソ連崩壊 Soviet Union dissolved	宮澤喜一 Miyazawa Kiichi
	美浜原発事故 Mihama nuclear accident	
1992（平成4）	ボスニア・ヘルツェゴビナ内戦開始 Commencement of civil war in Bosnia-Herzegovina	
	PKO協力法成立 Law on Cooperation in U.N. Peacekeeping Operations passed	

	金丸信、献金問題発覚 Disclosure of questionable donations to Kanamaru Shin	
1993（平成5）	米大統領にクリントンが就任 Bill Clinton becomes U.S. president	
	連立政権の発足により、55年体制に終止符 Non-LDP coalition government formed, marking end of "1955 system"	細川護煕 Hosokawa Morihiro
1994（平成6）	松本サリン事件 Matsumoto Sarin Incident	羽田孜 Hata Tsutomu
	大江健三郎ノーベル文学賞受賞 Oe Kenzaburo receives Nobel Prize for literature	村山富市 Murayama Tomiichi
1995（平成7）	阪神・淡路大震災 Kobe earthquake	
	地下鉄サリン事件 Subway Sarin Gas Incident	
1996（平成8）	薬害エイズ事件、安部英逮捕 HIV-contaminated blood scandal, Abe Takeshi arrested	橋本龍太郎 （第1・2次） Hashimoto Ryutaro (1st, 2nd terms)
1997（平成9）	京都議定書採択 Kyoto Protocol to stop global warming	
1998（平成10）	英軍によるイラク空爆 U.S. military begins bombing of Iraq	小渕恵三 Obuchi Keizo
1999（平成11）	EUの単一通貨ユーロ導入 Introduction of euro as common currency of EU	
2000（平成12）	ロシア大統領にプーチン就任 Putin becomes president of Russia	森喜朗（第1・2次） Mori Yoshiro (1st, 2nd terms)
	白川英樹ノーベル化学賞受賞 Shirakawa Hideki receives Nobel Prize for chemistry	
2001（平成13）	米大統領にジョージ・W・ブッシュが就任 George W. Bush becomes U.S. president	小泉純一郎 （第1・2次） Koizumi Jun'ichiro (1st, 2nd terms)
	9・11米国同時多発テロ事件 9/11 Incident, terrorist attacks on U.S.	
2002（平成14）	小柴昌俊ノーベル物理学賞、田中耕一ノーベル化学賞受賞 Koshiba Masatoshi receives Nobel Prize for physics Tanaka Koichi receives Nobel Prize for chemistry	
2003（平成15）	BSE輸入牛肉疑惑発覚 Imports of beef suspended due to BSE outbreak	
	アジアでSARS流行 SARS outbreak in Asia	
2004（平成16）	新潟中越地震 Niigata earthquake	

	陸上自衛隊イラク復興支援に出発 SDF dispatched to Iraq to assist reconstruction	
	鳥インフルエンザ流行 Outbreak of avian flu	
2005（平成17）	京都議定書発効 Kyoto Protocol	
	衆議院、郵政解散 Lower House of Diet votes to break up postal services administration	小泉純一郎（第3次） Koizumi Jun'ichiro (3rd term)
2006（平成18）	ライブドア事件 Livedoor Incident	
2007（平成19）	郵政民営化に伴い、日本郵政公社が解散 Privatization of Japan Post	安倍晋三（第1次） Abe Shinzo (1st term)
2008（平成20）	北京五輪 Beijing Olympics	福田康夫 Fukuda Yasuo
2009（平成21）	アメリカ合衆国でオバマ大統領就任 Barack Obama is inaugurated as president	麻生太郎 Aso Taro
		鳩山由紀夫 Hatoyama Yukio
2010（平成22）	鈴木章・根岸英一ノーベル化学賞受賞 Suzuki Akira and Negishi Eiichi receive Nobel Prize in Chemistry	菅直人 Kan Naoto
2011（平成23）	東日本大震災、津波、原発災害 3.11 Earthquake, Tsunami and Nuclear Disaster	野田佳彦 Noda Yoshihiko
2012（平成24）	山中伸弥ノーベル医学賞受賞 Yamanaka Shinya receives Nobel Prize in Medicine	安倍晋三（第2次） Abe Shinzo (2nd term)
2013（平成25）	富士山、世界文化遺産に Mt. Fuji is registered as a cultural site of world heritage	
2014（平成26）	赤﨑勇・天野浩・中村修二がノーベル物理学賞を受賞 Akasaki Isamu, Amano Hiroshi, Nakamura Shuji receive Nobel Prize in Physics	安倍晋三（第3次） Abe Shinzo (3rd term)
2015（平成27）	梶田隆章がノーベル物理学賞、大村智がノーベル生理学・医学賞を受賞 Kajita Takaaki, Omura Satoshi receive Nobel Prize in Physiology or Medicine	
2016（平成28）	大隅良典がノーベル生理学・医学賞 Osumi Yoshinori receive Nobel Prize in Physilogy or Medicine	
	オバマ大統領が広島訪問 President Obama visits Hiroshima	

2017 (平成29)	アメリカ合衆国でドナルド・トランプが大統領就任 Donald Trump is inaugurated as president	
	核兵器禁止条約が国際連合総会で採択 Nuclear Weapons Convention adopted at United Nations General Assembly	
2018 (平成30)	ドナルド・トランプと金正恩による初の米朝首脳会談 First U.S.-North Korea summit between Donald Trump and Kim Jong-un	
	日産のカルロス・ゴーン会長が逮捕される Nissan Chairman Carlos Ghosn is arrested	
2019 (令和元)	元号が平成から令和になる Reiwa era begins	
	吉野彰がノーベル化学賞受賞 Yoshino Akira receives Nobel Prize in Chemistry	
	消費税の税率が10パーセントになる Sales tax rate becomes 10 percent	
2020 (令和2)	新型コロナウィルスの流行により世界中で様々なイベントが中止・延期になる New coronavirus outbreak causes cancellation and postponement of various events around the world	菅義偉 Suga Yoshihide
2021 (令和3)	前年に延期になった東京オリンピック開催 Hosting the Tokyo Olympics postponed from the previous year	岸田文雄 Kishida Fumio
2022 (令和4)	ロシアがウクライナに侵攻 Russia invades Ukraine	
	安倍元首相が銃撃され死亡 Former Prime Minister Abe shot and killed	

英語索引　English Index

A

Abe Shinzo　249, 259

Abenomics　249

Aiko, Princess　217

AKB48　229

Akihito, Emperor　181, 257

Akishino, Prince　215, 257

Allied nations　33

Ampo　105

Anti-war Movement　107

Asama Lodge Incident　129

atomic bomb　23, 67

B

bad loans　201

Berlin Wall　183

big bang　201

black market　27, 31

bursting of the economic bubble　189

C

Chiang Kai-shek　21

China-Japan Peace and Friend-ship Treaty　121

Churchill　21

"Class A" criminals　65

Clean Government Party　145

COVID-19　251

D

Declaration of Humanity　47

Democratic Party of Japan 197, 249

Diaoyu Islands　247

dismantling of conglomer-ates　51

Disparate Society　225

distribution system　25

Doi Takeo　177

Dokdo Islands　247

Dulles, John Foster　77

F

Farm Land Reform Law　53

firebombing　23

flotation of the yen against the dollar　119

freeters　225

Fukushima Daiichi Nuclear Power Plant complex　241

full-time housewife　159

Fundamental Law of Education　55

G

General Headquarters/Supreme Commander of the Allied Powers　39

Gorbachev　181

Great East Japan Earthquake 239

H

Hatoyama Yukio   197

heir crisis   215

high-speed growth   91, 97, 133

Hisahito (of Akishino), Prince
215, 219, 257

Horiemon phenomenon   207

Hosokawa Morihiro   89, 181

I

Ichikawa Fusae   147

Ikeda Hayato   75, 95

immigrant labor   179

Imperial Household   215, 217,
219

imperial conferences   69

Income-Doubling Plan   95

industrial pollution   99

Ishihara Shintaro   247

IT bubble   205

it hurts disease (*itai-itai byo*)
103

J

Japan Socialist Party (JSP)   89,
145

Japanese Constitution   47

Japanese Constitution, article 9
45, 47, 63, 79, 133

K

Kadena base   109

Kan Naoto   197

Kanemaru Shin   197

karoshi   159

Kiko, Princess   215

Koizumi Jun'ichiro   203, 217

Korean Conflict   73

Kurosawa Akira   7, 85, 87

L

labor unions   51, 57, 59, 137

Law on Cooperation in United
Nations Peacekeeping Operations   185

Lehman Shock   219, 223

Liberal Democratic Party (LDP)
89, 105, 141, 143, 145, 151,
179, 181, 195, 197, 249, 259

Livedoor   207, 209, 211

Lockheed Aircraft Corporation   145

lost decade   225

M

MacArthur, Douglas   35, 37,
39, 43, 47, 61, 63, 77

Masako, Princess   215, 217

meltdown   241

mergers and acquisitions   209

Minamata disease   101

Ministry of International Trade
and Industry (MITI)   97

Mishima Yukio   125, 127, 131

Miyazaki Hayao   213

Momoiro Clover Z   235, 237

multination expedition   183

multiple-generation
families   93

N

Naruhito, Crown Prince   217,
219, 257

National Police Reserve   63

Nixon, Richard 117, 119
Nixon Shocks 117

O

Ohtani Shohei 261
Oil Shock 123, 125, 163, 223
Okamoto Taro 171
Onoda Hiroo 129, 131
Ooka Shohei 87
Organization of Petroleum Exporting Countries (OPEC) 123
Osaka Expo 171

P

pandemic 251
Peace Treaty 77, 79, 83
perestroika 181
Persian Gulf War 183
Plaza Accord 191
Pokémon 211
Pollution Countermeasures Basic Law 103
Potsdam Declaration 19, 21, 23
privatization of Japan National Railway 201
privatization of postal services 203
privatize the three major public corporations 181
public works 143, 147, 149

Q

quick profits 93

R

Recruit Cosmos 197

red purge 59
remote work 253
restructuring 189
reverse course 57, 59
Reversion of Okinawa 113, 133

S

san-chan farming 151
sarariiman 159
Self-Defense Forces (SDF) 63, 65, 125, 183, 185
Senkaku Islands 245, 247
Shinkansen 99, 117
6-3-3 system 55
soil liquefaction 241
Soviet–Japanese Joint Declaration 83
spiritual sales 261
Stalin 21
subprime loan crisis 221
Supreme Commander of the Allied Powers (SCAP) 37, 39, 41, 47, 51, 55, 57, 59, 61, 71, 75, 77, 83
system of 1955 89, 181

T

Takeshima 245, 247
Takeshita Noboru 195, 197
Tanaka Kakuei 121, 141, 143, 145
Tanaka Yasuo 171
telecommuting 253
Territorial Dispute 245
three sacred treasures (*sanshu no jingi*) 95
Tiananmen Square Incident 181

Tojo Hideki   33, 65, 129

Tokyo Olympic Games   107, 115

Tokyo War Crimes Trial   65

Trade Friction   137

trinity reform   205

troubles at Todai   113, 115

Truman   21, 67, 77

tsunami   239, 241, 245, 257

two-party political arrangement (system)   89, 197, 199

U

U-2 Incident   133

unconditional surrender   19

Unification Church   259

(United States–Japan) Security Treaty   81, 105, 107, 109, 113, 127, 135

Uno Sosuke   197

V

vaccinations   255

Vietnam War   99, 107, 109, 113, 127

Voices of the Ocean   85

Y

Yamagami Tetsuya   259

Yamaichi Securities   195

Yokoi Shoichi   129, 131

Yoshida Shigeru   73, 75, 79

日本語索引 Japanese Index

あ

愛子内親王　216

ITバブル　204

秋篠宮悠仁　214, 218, 256

秋篠宮文仁　214, 218, 256

明仁天皇　256

あさま山荘事件　124, 126, 128

安倍晋三　199, 248, 258

アベノミクス　248, 250

安保　104

池田勇人　74, 94, 198

諫早湾干拓事業　149

石原慎太郎　246

イタイイタイ病　102

市川房枝　144

魚釣島　246

失われた10年　224

宇野宗佑　196, 199

A級戦犯　64, 68

AKB48　228

液状化現象　240

NTT　180

M&A（合併・買収）　208

オイルショック　122, 124, 162, 222

大岡昇平　86

大阪万博　28, 170, 172

大谷翔平　260

大手公社の民営化　180

岡本太郎　170

沖縄返還　112, 132, 134

小野田寛郎　130

OPEC（石油輸出国機構）　122

か

外国人労働者　178

核家族　92

格差社会　224

勝ち組、負け組　224

嘉手納基地　108

金丸信　196

「カムカム英語」　25

過労死　158

為替レート　60, 118, 188

川端康成　213

感染爆発　250

菅直人　196, 199

『きけわだつみのこえ』　84

紀子妃　214

金日成（キム・イルソン）　76, 127

逆コース　56, 58

教育基本法　54

玉音放送　22, 24

黒澤明　6, 84, 86

経済安定9原則　60

警察予備隊　62, 64

原子爆弾（原爆）　22, 62, 66, 68, 82

小泉純一郎　180, 199, 202, 216

皇位継承の危機　214

公害対策基本法　102

公共事業　142, 146, 148, 196

皇室典範　216, 256

公職追放　40

皇太子徳仁　214, 218

高度経済成長　90, 170

公明党　144

講和条約　76, 78, 80, 82

国民皆保険制度　165

55年体制　88, 180

御前会議　68

ゴルバチョフ　180

さ

在宅勤務　252

財閥解体　50

サザエさん　28, 29

サブプライム・ローン問題　220

サラリーマン　28, 158, 160, 162, 218, 224

三種の神器　94

三ちゃん農業　150

三位一体改革　204

GHQ（連合国軍最高司令官総司令部）　38, 40, 42, 44, 45, 46, 50, 54, 56, 58, 60, 70, 74, 76, 82

JR　172, 180

自衛隊　64, 124, 126, 182, 184

JT　180

下山事件　60, 61

自由民主党（自民党）　88, 104, 140, 142, 144, 150, 178, 180, 187, 194, 196, 198, 199, 248, 258

ジュリアナ東京　168, 169

焼夷弾　22

蒋介石　20

食料自給率　152, 153

ジョセフ・マッカーシー　60, 62, 63

所得倍増計画　94

新型コロナウイルス　250

新幹線開通　116

スターリン　20

石油輸出国機構（OPEC）　122

尖閣諸島　244, 246

専業主婦　158

た

竹下登　194, 196, 198

竹島　244, 246

多国籍軍　182

田中角栄　120, 140, 141, 142, 144, 198

田中康夫　170

谷崎潤一郎　212, 213

ダレス　78

チャーチル　20

朝鮮戦争　72, 76, 77, 84, 96

通商産業省　96

津波　238, 240, 244

天安門事件　180

天皇　18, 22, 24, 36, 42, 44, 46, 48, 49, 66, 68, 70, 114, 130, 180, 214, 216, 256

天皇の地方御巡幸　49

土居健郎　176

統一教会（旧）　258

東京オリンピック　106, 114, 115, 250

東京裁判　64,68

東条英機　32,64,128

東大紛争　112,114

特需　72,92,96,98

ドッジライン　60

トルーマン　20,66,76,77

な

二・一ゼネスト　58

ニクソン・ショック　116

二大政党制　88,198

日米安全保障条約　80,104,126,
134

『日米会話手帳』　24,25

日ソ共同宣言　82

日中共同声明　120

日中平和友好条約　120

（日本国）憲法　32,42,44,45,46,
62,78,132,182,187,258

（日本国憲法）第9条　44,46,62,
64,78,132

日本社会党　88,144,187,198,199

人間宣言　46,49

農地改革　50,52

は

パール判事　68

配給制度　24

派遣切り　222

鳩山由紀夫　196,199

バブル（経済）　168,169,178,188,
192,200,204,208,224,226

反戦運動　106

万博　28,170,172

PKO協力法（国際連合平和維持活
動等に対する協力に関する法律）
184

東日本大震災　238,248,256

（金融）ビッグバン　200

福島第一原子力発電所　240,244

プラザ合意　190

フリーター　224

不良債権　194,200,202

粉飾決算　208

ベアテ・シロタ・ゴードン　44

ベトナム戦争　96,106,108,112

ベルリンの壁　180,182

ペレストロイカ　180

変動相場制　118

貿易摩擦　136,138

ポケモン　210

細川護熙　88,180,199

ポツダム宣言　18,20,22

ホリエモン　206

ま

雅子妃　216

マッカーサー　34,36,38,42,46,
60,62,76,77

マッカーシズム　62,63

松川事件　61

三島由紀夫　124,126,213

三鷹事件　61

水俣病　100,102

宮崎駿　212

民主党　196,198,199,248

（無条件）降伏　18,20,22,24,34,
76

村上春樹　213

メルトダウン　240

ももいろクローバーZ　234
桃太郎　54

や

山一證券　194
山上徹也　258
ヤミ市　20, 26, 28, 30
郵政民営化　180, 202
U2偵察機　132, 134
横井庄一　128, 130
吉田茂　58, 72, 74, 78, 198
吉本ばなな　213
よど号ハイジャック事件　126

ら

ライブドア　206, 208, 210
リーマン・ショック　218, 222
リクルートコスモス　194

リストラ　188, 192, 222
リモートワーク　252
領土問題　244, 246
霊感商法　266
レッド・パージ　40, 58, 60
連合国　20, 22, 32, 66, 68, 76
連合国軍最高司令官　36, 76
連合国軍最高司令官総司令部
　（GHQ）　38, 40, 42, 44, 45, 46,
　50, 54, 56, 58, 60, 70, 74, 76, 82
労働組合　46, 50, 56, 58, 60, 74,
　104, 136
6-3-3制　54
ロッキード事件　140

わ

ワクチン接種　254
湾岸戦争　182

参考文献　Bibliography

Allinson, Gary D. *Japan's Postwar History*. 2nd ed. Ithaca: Cornell University Press, 2004.

Bix, Herbert P. *Hirohito and the Making of Modern Japan*. New York: HarperCollins, 2000.

Chugoku Kankoku no rekishi kyokasho ni kakareta Nippon. Tokyo: Bessatsu Takarajima, 2005.

Curtis, Gerald L. *Japan's Foreign Policy after the Cold War: Coping with Change*. Armonk, NY: M.E. Sharpe, 1993.

Dower, John W. *Embracing Defeat: Japan in the Wake of World War II*. New York, W.W. Norton & Company, 1999.

Fowler, Edward. "Rendering Words, Traversing Cultures: On the Art and Politics of Translating Modern Japanese Fiction." *Journal of Japanese Studies* 18:1 (1992), pp. 1–44.

Goodby, James E., Vladimir I. Ivanov, Nobuo Shimotomai. *"Northern Territories" and Beyond: Russian, Japanese and American Perspectives*. Westport, CT: Praeger, 1995.

Gordon, Andrew. *A Modern History of Japan: From Tokugawa Times to the Present*. New York: Oxford University Press, 2003.

—— (ed.). *Postwar Japan as History*. Berkeley: University of California Press, 1993.

Green, Michael J. *Japan's Reluctant Realism: Foreign Policy Challenges and Era of Uncertain Power*. New York: Palgrave, 2001.

Hane, Mikiso. *Eastern Phoenix: Japan Since 1945*. Boulder: Westview Press, 1996.

Hanneman, Mary L. *Japan Faces the World: 1925–1952*. Harlow: Pearson Education Limited, 2001.

Ikegami, Akira. *So datta no ka! Nihon Gendai-shi*. Tokyo: Shueisha, 2001.

Irokawa, Daikichi. *The Age of Hirohito: In Search of Modern Japan*. trans. Mikiso Hane and John K. Urda. New York: Free Press, 1995.

Japan Economic Foundation. *Japan Spotlight: Economy, Culture & History*. 2004–2005.

Kalat, David. *A Critical History and Filmography of Toho's Godzilla Series*. Jefferson, NC, and London: McFarland & Company, Inc., 1997.

Kingston, Jeffrey. *Japan in Transformation: 1952–2000*. Harlow: Pearson Education Limited, 2001.

LaFeber, Walter. *The Clash: A History of U.S.–Japan Relations*. New York and London: W. W. Norton, 1997.

Large, Stephen S., ed. *Showa Japan: Political, economic and social history: 1926–1989*. London and New York: Routledge, 1998. Four volumes.

Material has also been used from issues of *Japan Spotlight*, *The Journal of Japanese Studies*, and *Monumenta Nipponica* as well as the websites of BBC News, CNN, *Time* and *The Economist*.

McCargo, Duncan. *Contemporary Japan*. 2nd ed. New York: Palgrave Macmillan, 2004.

McClain, James L. *Japan: A Modern History*. New York and London: W. W. Norton and Company, 2002.

McCormack, G. *The Emptiness of Japanese Affluence*. Armonk, NY: M.E. Sharpe, 1996.

Totman, Conrad. *A History of Japan*, 2nd ed. Oxford: Blackwell Publishing, 2005.

Treat, John Whittier (ed.). *Contemporary Japan and Popular Culture*. Honolulu: University of Hawai'i Press, 1996.

Tsurumi Shunsuke, *A Cultural History of Postwar Japan, 1945–1980*. New York and London: KPI, 1987.

English Conversational Ability Test
国際英語会話能力検定

● E-CATとは…
英語が話せるようになるための
テストです。インターネット
ベースで、30分であなたの発
話力をチェックします。

www.ecatexam.com

● iTEP®とは…
世界各国の企業、政府機関、アメリカの大学
300校以上が、英語能力判定テストとして採用。
オンラインによる90分のテストで文法、リー
ディング、リスニング、ライティング、スピー
キングの5技能をスコア化。iTEP®は、留学、就
職、海外赴任などに必要な、世界に通用する英
語力を総合的に評価する画期的なテストです。

www.itepexamjapan.com

［対訳ニッポン双書］

日本現代史【改訂第3版】
Contemporary Japanese History: since 1945

2009年 9 月28日　　　　初版第1刷発行
2013年 9 月 4 日　　増補改訂版第1刷発行
2024年 3 月 9 日　　改訂第3版第1刷発行

著　者　　ジェームス・M・バーダマン

監訳者　　樋口謙一郎

発行者　　浦　　晋　亮

発行所　　IBCパブリッシング株式会社
　　　　　〒162-0804 東京都新宿区中里町29番3号 菱秀神楽坂ビル
　　　　　Tel. 03-3513-4511　Fax. 03-3513-4512
　　　　　www.ibcpub.co.jp

印刷所　　株式会社シナノパブリッシングプレス

© ジェームス・M・バーダマン 2024
© IBC パブリッシング 2024
Printed in Japan

ISBN978-4-7946-0804-8